The Power Pressure Cooker XL Cookbook

Cookbook

123 Delicious Electric Pressure Cooker Recipes For The Whole Family

WHITLEY FOX

ISBN-13: 978-1541009004

ISBN-10: 1541009002

DEDICATION

To Merry, you make my dreams come true.

TABLE OF CONTENTS

INTRODUCTION

Pressure Cookers

Pressure cookers help to prepare wonderfully delicious foods in ways that save time and effort. They are convenient, easy to use and energy-efficient — using far less energy than many other appliances. A pressure cooker is simply a special airtight cooking pot that cooks foods faster by containing steam in a preset pressure. They make use of high pressures and high temperatures to expedite the cooking activity and to retain the nutritious content of foods.

Pressure cooking involves using the sealed steam in a pressure cooker to cook food. The sealed liquid such as broth, water or wine, traps the steam that rises from the liquid, raising the pressure inside the pressure cooker and the maximum temperature of the liquid to as high as 248° F (120° C). This is far much higher than the maximum heat you can possibly get from cooking in an ordinary saucepan. The higher temperature from pressure cooking penetrates food quickly, reduces cooking time and retains more nutrients and vitamins in your food. Pressure cooking is totally different from other kinds of cooking as it comes with its own procedures and languages. First, you will have to heat up the pressure cooker, add in the ingredients, cover the lid securely and let it cook for a particular amount of time, at a certain pressure level before releasing the pressure.

A Bit Of History...

The pressure cooker was invented in 1679 by a Frenchman, Denis Papin. He was a physicist who wanted to show how pressure and steam, new physics discoveries, can be translated into cooking. His pot, "Digester", wasn't very safe for high pressure cooking and it was many years later, precisely during World War II that pressure cooking became a household cooking method with the stovetop pressure cookers. This was so because people needed to save fuel, cook faster and cook cheaper cuts of meat easily.

The stovetop pressure cooker had a safety valve, a steam regulator, and pressure-activated interlock mechanism to help guard against overheating and explosion. Once a pre-set pressure is attained during cooking, the internal pressure pushes up the steam regulator to allow the steam to escape. This is why they often produce a loud hissing noise when the pressure is on.

The Electric Pressure Cooker was invented about 2 decades ago. It consists of a cooking pot, the electric heating element, and the temperature / pressure sensors. An internal micro-processor controls the heating process through the readings of the temperature and pressure sensors. Historians aren't sure about the actual date of invention as well as the original inventors but a Chinese scientist, Mr. Yong-Guang Wang, officially filed the first electric pressure cooker patent on January 9th, 1991.

After a period of time, manufacturers of top electric pressure cooker began to combine various cooking pressure, temperature and time duration to come up with different cooking profiles such as steaming, rice cooking, braising, simmering, slow cooking, stewing and warming. This combination led to new inventions of electric pressure cooker— the programmable multi-cooker. To guarantee the safety of these pressure, better manufacturing standards and technology was developed. Safety locks, pressure regulators portable cookers and low-pressure fryers are such examples.

The most appealing thing about the electric pressure cooker is its 'set and forget' feature. Simply set it and go about your business. Since it is highly automated, you only need to select the pressure you need from a range of

2

multiple settings and let it do its work. It also has a timer that indicates when the food is done. Additionally, most electric cookers, including the Power Pressure Cooker will switch over to a 'keep warm' mode when the cooking time is done. Consequently, cooking is easier, even for a first-time user.

The Power Pressure Cooker XL

The Power Pressure Cooker XL is highly efficient — using the power pressure of steam to cook so quickly and so richly. Meat and seafood retain their intense flavor without added fat; vegetables come out tender-crisp, with their fiber intact. Power Cooking is the modern-day answer to pressure cooking your favorite homemade meals with just the push of a button. It locks in essential nutrients and vitamins in food. Indeed, the pressure cooker is the secret to incredibly fast and yummy meals.

The Power Pressure Cooker XL comes in two models: the Power Cooker XL and Power Cooker XL Pro, the latter being more popular. It has an intelligent one-touch preset buttons settings for cooking fish, meat, vegetables, rice, beans, soup or stews and so much more. These cooking modes may either be used alone or combined to produce an endless range of results. To pressure cook your special beef stew, for instance, just add in your ingredients and push the Stew button, and watch the Power Pressure Cooker get to work!

The Power Pressure Cooker XL can also perform various functions such as browning, steaming, slow cooking and even canning! It has additional settings to aid the most common cooking tasks such as *Keep Warm* to keep food at the right temperature for those who cannot make it to the table on time. Its *Select time*, *time adjustment* and *delay timer* functions are highly beneficial.

Cooking In Your Power Pressure Cooker XL

Once you select your desired cook mode button, a default time for that mode button will show on the digital display. But, before the countdown clock begins its work, the Power pressure cooker must attain full pressure and this can take up to 17 minutes. Remember to factor this in for all the recipes you want to cook. However, you can override the default or pre-programmed cook time by pressing the *Time Adjustment button* and it will change in 1-minute increments. The *Select Button* is helpful when you want to select a specific time range from the 3 available time options on your manual. By selecting the *Delay timer* function, you can cook your meal at a later time.

If you have frozen foods, you do not need to defrost before cooking. Simply add an extra ten minutes of cooking time.

<u>Sautéing or Browning</u>

Sautéing involves cooking food quickly and lightly in a few spoons of oil, butter or fat. A sauté pan is brought to temperature over medium-high heat, and then thin or small pieces of food, such as onions and garlic, are quickly added and sautéed to bring out their delightful aroma. In your Power Pressure Cooker XL, you only need to press any of the preset buttons and this will brown your food, usually meat, to increase its delicious flavors and aromas. Remember to always sauté with the lid off.

Slow Cooking

Slow cooking is a "set and forget" cooking method. Simply put something up the morning and by evening, you have a great meal waiting for you. It saves lots of time and energy. You can enjoy succulent, slow-cooked meals prepared quickly and with great flavor. Slow cooking is perfect for soups, stews and meats. It is also economical, because it helps to cook cheaper cuts of meat succulently. Use the Slow Cook feature of your Power Cooker XL, with its low pressure, to great advantage.

Rice -Cooking

The rice cooker function of the Power Pressure Cooker XL is just great! While it has a Rice setting, it also has 3 individual sub settings for White Rice, Brown Rice, and Wild Rice. These settings are program specifically for each rice type with its time and pressure. Simply add the rice, water and other ingredients, secure the lid and press the button. A minimum of 6 minutes later, you have a delicious and fluffy rice meal to enjoy. There is no need to bother about remembering to stir or to constantly check to prevent burning. Power Pressure Cooker XL makes rice-cooking so easy.

Steaming

In steaming, the steam from the cooking liquid is used to cook the food. To steam, add water to the pressure cooker, insert the steamer tray, and then add the food to be steamed on top of the tray. The resulting steam from the heated water cooks the food in only 2 minutes! Steaming is perfect for vegetables, they become tender when steamed but still retain their nutrients and color.

Canning

You can now can your preferred fruits and vegetables. The required pressure for canning is 80-kPa/11.6 psi and this can be attained by the Power Cooker XL.

Keep Warm

After the set cooking time elapses, the unit will automatically switch to the *Keep Warm* mode to keep your food warm until you are ready to enjoy it. However, try not to keep foods longer than 4 hours so they do not lose their flavor and texture.

Pressure Release

To quick release pressure, you must switch the pressure release valve to open when the program ends. For natural release, you simply press *Cancel* and let the pressure come down on its own, before opening the lid.

Pressure Cooking Tips

The Power Pressure Cooker XL can be cook virtually anything— from main courses to desserts, all kind of meats, rice, diverse vegetables and potatoes. Nevertheless, here are a few basic tips to remember:

- Follow the manufacturer's instructions concerning amount of liquid to add to your cooker. This is important.
- When adapting traditional recipes to your pressure cooker, add less liquid but more spices and herbs.

- Don't fill any pressure cooker with too much food. Never fill a pressure cooker more than two-thirds full with food. Also, never pack food tightly into a pressure cooker.
- Cut foods in even-sized pieces to enable them cook at the same amount of time.
- Remember that pressure-cooked foods are usually hotter than food cooked by other methods so handle carefully.
- Never let water get into the appliance and always unplug it before cleaning.
- Remove the lid only when all pressure is released. Do not force it open if you are finding it difficult to open; as this signifies that that the cooker is still pressurized.

Benefits & Advantages

- **Enhancing The Richness And Natural Flavors Of Foods**

Get more nutritional boost from pressure cooked foods. The longer foods are cooked, the more nutrients are destroyed; but, with shorter cooking times, your foods will not sit in boiling water for too long. Consequently, you can be sure your foods will not lose their vitamins and taste, color and flavor. Pressure cooking helps to retain moisture in foods, which results in more concentrated flavors. The liquids can also be added to your meals for you to enjoy their residual nutrients.

- **Save On Preparation Time**

Foods cook up to 70% faster with automatic pressure cookers. This way, you can cook faster and save on preparation time. If you need to get something quick and tasty for dinner, you can whip up tasty foods in the nick of time and enjoy quality time with your family.

- **Convenience Of One Pot Cooking**

When you come home late from the office or you are tired after a long day's work, the convenience of a one-pot cooking will make your life easier. Just throw in all your ingredients, press some buttons and let the Power pressure Cooker XL get to work. By the time you are through tidying up the kitchen and getting the table set, dinner will be ready. Wonderfully convenient!

- **Conserves Energy**

You only need one pot- and not multiple pots on separate burners to cook your meals. This helps you to save a significant amount on energy. Besides, foods require less cooking, so you can save up to 70% of energy by pressure cooking. Less heat and less time means this very high percentage of energy savings over other types of cooking. This helps to reduce the size of your monthly electricity bill.

- **Clean & Pleasant**

Electric Pressure cookers contain splatters effectively. So no more splatters on your stove top or spillovers in the oven. Additionally, it is totally quiet, and produces no steam, smells or excessive kitchen heat.

- **Easy Cleanup**

Since there are no splashes, boils, splatters or steam escaping from your Power Pressure Cooker XL, (as long as the lid is secure), clean-up is easier. More so, there's only one pot to clean!

- **Cooler Kitchen**

Cooking in a stovetop or oven generates heat and steam, making you sweat and uncomfortable during cooking. However, in pressure cooking, heat and steam cannot escape as the pressure cookers retain them. You can now cook any meals you want, especially those that being reserved for colder months.

BREAKFAST & BRUNCH RECIPES

Power Cooked Breakfast Quinoa

A perfect and healthy way to start your day is to take this light and fluffy quinoa, served with sliced almonds and fresh berries.

Servings: 6

Preparation time: 1 minute

Cook time: 2 minutes

Ingredients

1 1/2 cups uncooked quinoa

1/4 teaspoon ground cinnamon

2 tablespoons of maple syrup

1/2 teaspoon vanilla

2 1/4 cups of water

A pinch of salt

Milk, fresh berries and sliced almonds, for toppings

Directions

1. Rinse the quinoa well then add it to the inner pot of the Power Cooker, together with water, vanilla, maple syrup, cinnamon, and salt.

2. Place the lid on, lock it and switch the pressure release valve to closed. Set it on STEAM mode (2 mins). Once the program ends, the cooker will switch to Keep Warm by itself. Turn the pressure release valve to open. Wait until the steam is released completely before opening the cover.

3. Fluff the quinoa. Enjoy hot with milk, sliced almonds and berries.

Homemade Applesauce

This delicious homemade applesauce goes well on steel cut oatmeal. It can also be taken as a snack.

Servings: 6

Preparation time: 2minutes

Cook time: 2minutes

Ingredients

3 lbs. apples, peeled, cored& quartered

¾ teaspoon of ground cinnamon

1/3 cup of apple juice, unsweetened

Directions

1. Combine all ingredients in the Power Cooker.

2. Secure lid and switch the pressure release valve to closed. Set it on STEAM mode (2mins). Once the program ends, the cooker will switch to Keep Warm automatically.

3. Turn the pressure release valve to open. Wait until the steam is released completely before opening the cover.

4. Serve warm or cold.

Fruity Irish Oatmeal

If you want different flavors, substitute other dried fruit like cherries, dates and prunes.

Servings: 2

Preparation time: 5 minutes

Cook time: 8 minutes

Ingredients:

1 cup toasted steel-cut oats

3 cups of water, divided

1 cup apple juice

2 teaspoons butter

1 tablespoon apricots, snipped dried

1 tablespoon maple syrup

1 pinch salt

1 tablespoon golden raisins

1 tablespoon cranberries, dried

1/4 teaspoon ground cinnamon

To serve:

Chopped toasted nuts (pecans, walnuts), maple syrup, milk

Directions:

1. Place the steamer tray in the inner pot of the Power Cooker then pour 1/2 cup of water in.

2. In a metal bowl that can fit into the inner pot, add together 2 1/2 cups water, oats, butter, apple juice, cinnamon, maple syrup, raisins, apricots,

cranberries, and salt, stirring well to blend, then place the bowl on the metal tray.

3. Place the lid on, lock it and switch the pressure release valve to closed. Choose RICE/RISOTTO (6mins). Once the program ends, the cooker will switch to Keep Warm by itself.

4. Turn the pressure release valve to open. Wait until the steam is released completely before opening the cover. Using tongs, remove the metal bowl from the Power Cooker.

5. Spoon into bowls and top with maple syrup, chopped toasted nuts (pecans, walnuts) and milk.

Apple Buckwheat Cobbler
Servings: 4

Preparation time: 2 minutes

Cook time: 10 minutes

Ingredients

3- 3.5 lbs. raw apples, cut into chunks

½ cup medjool dates, chopped

½ cup dry buckwheat

2 teaspoon cinnamon

¼ tsp nutmeg

1 ½ cups of water

¼ teaspoon of powdered ginger

Directions

1. Put all the ingredients in the Power Cooker, stirring well to mix.

2. Cover and lock lid and then switch the pressure release valve to closed. Press SOUP/STEW (10mins). Once the timer gets to 0, the cooker will switch to Keep Warm automatically.

3. Switch the pressure release valve to open in order to release the steam. Remove the lid when the steam is fully released.

4. Serve warm or cold.

Cheesy Sausage Scramble

This goes well with toasted whole grain bread.

Servings: 8

Preparation time: 20 minutes

Cooking time: 27 minutes

Ingredients:

1 pound ground sausage

1 tablespoon vegetable oil

1/4 cup water

1 yellow bell pepper, seeded, diced

1 large sweet onion, diced

1 red bell pepper, seeded & diced

1 (1-pound) bag frozen hash browns, thawed

1 green bell pepper, seeded &diced

8 large eggs

Salt, to taste

1/2 pound grated Cheddar cheese

Freshly ground pepper, to taste

Directions:

1. Insert the inner pot in the Power Cooker. Set on CHICKEN/MEAT mode; heat oil and then add onion and bell peppers. Cook and stir it for 5 minutes. Once the onion is translucent, add the hash browns and sausage, stirring well.

2. Place the lid on, lock it and switch the pressure release valve to closed. Choose CANCEL. Press the button for RICE/RISOTTO and adjust to 8 minutes cooking time.

3. Once the program ends, the cooker will switch to Keep Warm by itself. Turn the pressure release valve to open. Wait until the steam is released completely before opening the cover. Drain any excess fat.

3. Whisk together eggs, water, salt and pepper and then pour over the potato-sausage mixture in the Power Cooker. Press "sauté, brown or steam" and then scramble the eggs and stir until they start to set.

4. Add in the cheese and keep scrambling until eggs are cooked and the cheese has melted. Serve immediately.

Blueberry Croissant Pudding
Perfect for a brunch, this recipe comes with a fresh delightful twist.

Servings: 10

Preparation time: minutes

Cook time: 20 minutes

Ingredients

1 cup blueberries, fresh or frozen

3 large croissants, cut (5 to 5 1/2 cups)

1- 8-ounce cream cheese, softened

2 eggs

2/3 cup sugar

1 cup of milk

1 teaspoon of vanilla

Directions

1. Place the croissants in the Power Cooker and add the blueberries. Whisk together the eggs, cream cheese, vanilla and sugar in a bowl until well mixed. Add the milk and mix thoroughly.

2. Pour the egg mixture over the croissants and then let it sit 20 minutes. Cover and lock the Power Cooker, and then switch the pressure release valve to closed. Select SOUP/STEW and adjust time to 20 minutes.

3. Once the timer gets to 0, the cooker will switch to Keep Warm by itself. Switch the pressure release valve to open in order to release the steam. Remove the lid when the steam is fully released.

4. Serve, topped with powdered sugar.

Apple & Cherry Breakfast Risotto
Delicious, creamy and nutritious, this breakfast recipe is also quick and easy to prepare.

Servings: 4

Preparation time: 2 minutes

Cook time: 10 minutes

Ingredients

1 1/2 cups Arborio rice

2 tablespoon of butter

2 large apples, cored & diced

1/3 cup brown sugar

1 1/2 tsp cinnamon

1 cup apple juice

1/2 cup dried cherries

3 cups milk

1/4 tsp salt

Directions

1. Melt the butter using the CHICKEN/MEAT mode. Add the rice, cook for 3 to 4 minutes, stirring constantly. Add the apples, brown sugar, spices, juice and milk and then stir.

2. Place the lid on, lock it and switch the pressure release valve to closed. Set it on RICE/RISOTTO mode (6 mins). Once the program ends, the cooker will switch to Keep Warm by itself. Turn the pressure release valve to open. Wait until the steam is released completely before opening the cover.

3. Remove rice from the cooker and stir in the cherries gently. Serve hot, topped with almonds and milk.

Egg Muffins Delight

Servings: 4

Preparation time: minutes

Cook time: minutes

Ingredients

4 eggs

4 tablespoon cheddar/Jack cheese, shredded

4 slices precooked bacon, crumbled

1 green onion, diced

1/4 tsp lemon pepper seasoning

1 ½ cups of water

Directions

1. Place a steamer tray in the bottom of Power Cooker and add water. Add together the eggs and lemon pepper in a large bowl and beat well.

2. Grease 4 small ramekins lightly with olive oil. Divide the bacon, cheese and green onion evenly into the ramekins. Pour the eggs into the ramekins, stirring gently. Place the ramekins on the steamer tray.

3. Place the lid on, lock it and switch the pressure release valve to closed. Select RICE/RISOTTO and adjust cooking time to 8 minutes. When the program is done, release the pressure by turning the pressure release valve to open, then open the lid.

BEEF MAIN DISHES

Lamb Rack Casserole

Servings: 6-8

Preparation time: 10 minutes

Cook time: 30 minutes

Ingredients

1 pound of baby potatoes

1 pound rack of lamb

2 medium size tomatoes

2 teaspoon of paprika

2 carrots

2 stalks of celery

1 large onion

3-4 large cloves of garlic

2 cups of chicken stock

3 table spoons of sherry or red wine

2 teaspoon of cumin powder

2 tablespoons of ketchup

A pinch of dried oregano leaves

A pinch of dried rosemary

A splash of beer

1-2 teaspoons of salt

Directions

1. Wash all vegetables; cut carrots and potatoes into 1 inch cubes. Dice the onion, garlic and tomatoes. Divide the rack of lamb into two.

2. Insert the inner pot in the Power Cooker. Add all ingredients to it. Place the lid on, lock it and switch the pressure release valve to closed.

3. Select the SOUP/STEW button, and adjust time to 30 minutes.

4. Once the timer gets to 0, the cooker will switch to Keep Warm automatically. Switch the pressure release valve to open so as to release the steam. Once all steam is released, remove the lid.

5. Serve and enjoy over rice.

Beef Burgundy

Rich, flavorful and oh so easy!

Servings: 6

Preparation time: 15minutes

Cook time: 30 minutes

Ingredients

1 1/2 lb London broil cut into cubes of 1 inch

32 oz of beef stock

4 tablespoon salted butter

1 tablespoon olive oil

8 tablespoon flour + 4 tablespoons cornstarch (Divide the flour in half. 4 for coating & 4 for thickening later)

1 teaspoon of salt

1 teaspoon of pepper

3/4 cup dry red wine

6 clove garlic left whole

2 teaspoons Worcestershire sauce

10 pearl onions, peeled

10 baby carrots left whole

Directions

1. Coat meat with cornstarch and 2 tablespoons flour, shaking off excess flour. Set meat aside for 10 minutes to coat well.

2. Put the inner pot inside the Power Cooker and then add the oil to it. Choose the CHICKEN/MEAT button to brown meat.

3. Add the broth, salt, pepper, wine, garlic, onions and carrots.

4. Place the lid on, lock it and switch the pressure release valve to closed. Press the button for the WARM/CANCEL setting.

5. Select SOUP/STEW and press the TIME ADJUSTMENT button to 25 minutes. Once the timer gets to 0, the cooker will switch to KEEP WARM by itself.

6. Switch the pressure release valve to open to release the steam. Once all steam is released, remove the lid and remove 1/2 cup of broth.

7. Add butter to the pot. Melt, and then whisk in the rest of the flour. Select SOUP/STEW. Add the reserved broth and whisk, to thicken, mixing well.

8. Add Worcestershire sauce and more salt or pepper, if necessary. Serve!

Hot Beef Chili

Servings: 4

Preparation time: 15 minutes

Cook time: 20 minutes

Ingredients:

2 lbs ground beef, 85% lean

4 cups tomatoes, crushed

1 large onion, peeled & diced

1/2 cup beef stock

1/3 cup dried black beans (soaked overnight)

1/3 cup dried red beans (soaked overnight)

1/3 cup dried navy beans (soaked overnight)

1 teaspoon cumin

1/4 cup chili powder

1 teaspoon ground coriander

1 tablespoon of sea salt

1 tablespoon of red pepper flakes, crushed

2 tablespoon of grape seed oil

1 tablespoon of sugar

Cheddar cheese for garnish

Sour cream for garnish

Directions

1. Place the inner pot inside the Power Cooker and then add the oil to it. Press the CHICKEN/MEAT button. Add the onions and beef then sauté for 5 minutes.

2. Add all the spices and cook another minute. Now add the rest of the ingredients.

3. Place the lid on, lock it and switch the pressure release valve to closed. Afterwards, press the button for the WARM/CANCEL setting.

4. Select SOUP/STEW and adjust time to 20 minutes. Once the timer gets to 0, the cooker will switch to Keep Warm automatically.

5. Switch the pressure release valve to open so as to release the steam. Once all steam is released, remove the lid.

6. Serve, garnished with sour cream and shredded cheddar cheese.

Beef &Porcini Mushroom Stew
Servings: 4-6

Preparation time: 15 minutes

Cook time: 20 minutes

Ingredients:

2 pounds beef chuck, cut into 1-inch cubes

1 tablespoon olive oil

1 medium red onion, diced roughly

1 rosemary sprig, de-stemmed & chopped (about 1 teaspoon)

1 celery stalk, sliced 1/2-inch pieces

1 cup beef stock, salt-free

1/4 teaspoon pepper

1/2 cup red wine (Sangiovese or Chianti)

1 teaspoon salt (reduce amount if using salted stock and butter)

1 oz dried porcini mushrooms, rinsed

2 large carrots, sliced into 1/2-inch rounds

2 tablespoons all-purpose flour

2 tablespoons unsalted butter

Directions

1. Place the inner pot inside the Power Cooker and then press the CHICKEN/MEAT button. Add the olive oil and brown the beef cubes for 5 minutes.

2. Add onions, rosemary, red wine, celery, stock, salt, and pepper, mixing well. Sprinkle the carrots and mushrooms over the stew mixture.

3. Close and lock lid and then switch the pressure release valve to closed. Select WARM/CANCEL.

4. Select CHICKEN/MEAT (15mins).

5. Once the timer gets to 0, the cooker will switch to Keep Warm automatically. Switch the pressure release valve to open to release the steam. Remove the lid when steam is fully released. Transfer the contents to a bowl.

6. Add butter to pot, melt and then drizzle with flour. Form into a paste and cook until the butter bubbles in the flour.

7. Add 6 tablespoons of the cooking liquid from the bowl and blend to loosen the paste. Pour all the contents of the bowl back into the Power Cooker and mix thoroughly then cover. Select WARM/CANCEL.

8. Select BEANS/LENTIL (5mins) to thicken.

9. Once thickened, release steam and remove lid. Serve and enjoy.

Beef Stroganoff

Servings: 4

Preparation time: 10 minutes

Cook time: 10 minutes

Ingredients:

2 lbs sliced beef, filet

1 lb mushrooms, cleaned &sliced

1 shallot, peeled & minced

1/4 cup sour cream

2 cups beef stock

1 bay leaf

1 sprig fresh thyme

3 tablespoons of butter

Directions

1. Place the inner pot inside the Power Cooker and then press the Select CHICKEN/MEAT button. Put the butter in it, add the meat, then brown.

2. Add the remaining ingredients except the sour cream.

3. Cover and lock the Power Cooker and then switch the pressure release valve to closed. Press the button for WARM/CANCEL.

4. Press the SOUP/STEW button. Once the timer gets to 0, the cooker will switch to Keep Warm automatically.

5. Switch the pressure release valve to open so as to release the steam. Remove the lid when steam is fully released.

6. Add the sour cream and stir well. Enjoy!

Italian Beef And Red Wine Sauce

Why go all the way to your local Italian restaurant when you can enjoy tender beef and pasta with minimal time and effort at home.

Servings: 4

Preparation time: 20 minutes

Cook time: 1hour: 5 minutes

Ingredients:

2 lb gravy beef, cut into pieces

1 tablespoon olive oil

2 carrots, peeled & finely chopped

2 celery sticks, trimmed & chopped

2 garlic cloves, finely chopped

1 brown onion, finely chopped

1/3 cup red wine

1 24-oz btl passata (tomato pasta sauce)

1 chicken stock cube

2 dried bay leaves

Pinch of white or raw sugar

1/3 cup boiling water

1 teaspoon dried oregano leaves

Cooked pasta, to serve

Finely grated parmesan, to serve

Directions

28

1. Pour the olive oil into the inner pot of the Power Cooker and Put in CHICKEN/MEAT mode. Add beef pieces and sauté. Transfer to a plate.

2. Add the celery, garlic, carrot and onion. Cook until soft.

3. Combine the beef, wine and passata in the pot. Dissolve the stock cube in the water and then add the stock, oregano, sugar and bay leaves. Season with salt and pepper. Stir well to combine.

4. Cover and lock lid and then switch the pressure release valve to closed. Select WARM/CANCEL.

5. Press the button for the SOUP/STEW mode and then adjust time to 40 Minutes. Once the timer gets to 0, the cooker will switch to Keep Warm mode by itself.

6. Switch the pressure release valve to open in order to release the steam. Remove the lid when the steam is fully released.

7. Remove beef, shred and return to pot. Stir well to combine. Add pasta and stir again to combine. Divide and serve, topped with parmesan.

Mediterranean Brisket in Power Cooker

Servings: 4

Preparation time: 20 minutes

Cook time: 1hour: 40 minutes

Ingredients:

2 1/2 lb Beef Brisket or London broil

1 lb baby carrots

1 teaspoon freshly ground pepper or seasoning

1 teaspoon salt

1 tbsp extra virgin olive oil

1 lb onions, peeled, sliced into 1/2 inch sizes lengthwise

12 oz white button or cremini mushrooms

3 clove garlic, peeled & chopped

1 teaspoon basil

1 teaspoon thyme

1 can (15 oz) diced tomatoes, drained

1/2 cup low-sodium beef broth

Directions

1. Score the meat's "fat cap" with a knife (do not remove the fat, though) and then season with salt and pepper on both sides.

2. In the inner pot of the Power Cooker, brown beef in olive oil using the CHICKEN/MEAT mode. Transfer to a plate. Place onions and garlic inside and sauté for 2 to 3 minutes. Add the mushrooms, basil and thyme. Cook and stir for 5 minutes.

3. Add the drained tomatoes and stock and then cook for 4 or 5 minutes. Add the browned brisket, add some of the vegetable mix and top with carrots.

4. Secure lid. Switch the pressure release valve to closed and press the button for WARM/CANCEL .Select CHICKEN/MEAT and press select time button set to 60 minutes.

5. Once the program ends, the cooker will switch to Keep Warm by itself. Turn the pressure release valve to open. Wait until the steam is released completely before opening the cover.

Lasagna Delight

Servings: 4

Preparation time: 15 minutes

Cook time: 20 minutes

Ingredients:

10 Meatballs, cooked & crushed

2 cups mozzarella, shredded

1/2 cup Parmigiano

2 cups ricotta cheese

3 eggs

1 teaspoon sea salt

3 tablespoons of parsley, chopped

1 teaspoon black pepper, freshly ground

1½ packs lasagna shells, pre-baked

3½cups tomato sauce

Directions

1. In a bowl, add together the ricotta cheese, 1cup mozzarella, parsley, pepper, salt, pepper and Parmigiano. Set to one side.

2. Place the inner pot in the Power Cooker. Pour a cup of tomato sauce and ½ cup of water.

3. Place 2 lasagna shells side by side in the centre. Break 2 shells in two along the length and fill in the sides.

4. Put half the meatballs on the shells then pour over ½ cup of sauce. Place another layer of shells and then add the ricotta cheese mixture.

5. Place down yet another layer of the lasagna shells and pour the remaining meatballs. Pour a cup of sauce on top of the crushed meatballs.

6. Place the last layer of shells and pour over a cup of sauce. Sprinkle over the mozzarella that's left on top.

7. Cover and lock the Power Cooker, and then switch the pressure release valve to closed.

8. Select SOUP/ STEW and then the button to adjust time until it reaches 20 minutes.

9. Once the timer gets to 0, the cooker will switch to Keep Warm by itself.

10. Switch the pressure release valve to open in order to release the steam. Remove the lid when the steam is fully released.

11. Set aside for about 10 minute to set up. Enjoy!

Nana's Pot Roast

Servings: 8

Preparation time: 10 minutes

Cook time: 40 minutes

Ingredients:

1 3-pound boneless chuck roast

2 stalks celery, diced

1 1-pound bag of baby carrots

1 large yellow onion, peeled & sliced

1 green bell pepper, seeded &diced

1 envelope onion soup mix

1 cup tomato juice

½ teaspoon black pepper

2 cloves garlic, peeled & minced

1 tablespoon steak sauce

1 tablespoon Worcestershire sauce

1 cup water

Directions

1. Cut the roast into serving-sized portions. Add the celery, green bell pepper, onion and carrots, to the inner pot of the Power Cooker.

2. Place the roast pieces on the vegetables and sprinkle with black pepper and soup mix.

3. Add the garlic, steak, Worcestershire sauce, tomato juice and water to a bowl; mix thoroughly and then pour into the pot.

4. Cover and lock lid and then switch the pressure release valve to closed.

5. Press the button for the SOUP/STEW and then adjust time to 40 Minutes. Once the timer gets to 0, the cooker will switch to Keep Warm mode by itself.

6. Switch the pressure release valve to open in order to release the steam. Remove the lid when the steam is fully released. Serve!

7. (This meal can be turned into 2 meals for 4 people the next day by making roast beef sandwiches. Refrigerating the leftovers in the pan juices will make the meat moist and tender).

Southern- Style Beef Roll-Ups

Servings: 6

Preparation time: 10 minutes

Cook time: 20 minutes

Ingredients:

1-1/2 pounds beef round steak, boneless, cut into 1/2 x 2-inch slices

1 can (15 ounces) black beans, rinsed & drained

1 teaspoon vegetable oil

1 small green pepper, sliced thinly

1 onion, thinly sliced

1 small red pepper, thinly sliced

1 teaspoon cumin

2 teaspoons chili powder

6 (8-inch) flour tortillas, warmed

1 can (14-1/2 ounces) stewed tomatoes, Mexican flavored

Toppings: chopped green onion, sour cream, chopped tomatoes, shredded Cheddar cheese

Directions

1. Pour vegetable oil into the inner pot in the Power Cooker. Set it to the CHICKEN/MEAT mode. Add the beef and brown.

2. Add peppers and onion and cook for 3 minutes. Add cumin, chili powder, black beans and stewed tomatoes.

3. Cover and lock, and then turn the pressure release valve to closed. Press the button for WARM/CANCEL.

34

4. Set it on CHICKEN/MEAT mode. Once the timer gets to 0, the cooker will switch to KEEP WARM.

5. Turn the pressure release valve to open. Remove lid once the steam is fully released.

6. Remove beef mixture using a slotted spoon and place in tortillas. Now, serve, garnished with toppings.

Flavorful Mongolian Beef
Servings: 6

Preparation time: 15 minutes

Cook time: 12 minutes

Ingredients:

2 lbs flank steak, cut into strips of 1/4"

4 cloves garlic, minced

1 tablespoon vegetable oil

1/2 cup soy sauce

2/3 cup dark brown sugar

1/2 cup water

1/2 teaspoon fresh ginger, minced

3 tablespoons of water

2 tablespoon cornstarch

3 green onions, sliced into 1-inch pieces

Directions

1. Season the beef with salt and pepper. Place the inner pot in the Power Cooker. Add oil to it and then press the CHICKEN/MEAT button. Add meat and brown. Transfer browned meat to a plate.

2. Add the garlic and cook for a minute. Add the soy sauce, brown sugar, ginger and1/2 cup water. Add browned beef and its juices.

3. Cover and lock the lid of the Power Cooker and switch the pressure release valve to closed. Select WARM/CANCEL.

4. Press the button for SOUP/STEW and then the Time button to get to 12 minutes. Once the timer gets to 0, the cooker will switch to KEEP WARM automatically.

5. Switch the pressure release valve to open in order to release the steam. Remove the lid when the steam is fully released.

6. Add together the cornstarch and 3 tablespoons of water and then whisk until smooth. Add the cornstarch mixture to the sauce in the Power Cooker.

7. Cover and lock. Cook to let it thicken for a while. Add green onions and enjoy.

Mini Rigatoni Bolognese
Servings: 4-6

Preparation time: 10 minutes

Cook time: 20 minutes

Ingredients:

1 lb ground beef

1 lb. mini rigatoni pasta

1 medium onion, peeled & chopped

2 cloves garlic, peeled and minced

2 tablespoons olive oil

1 medium carrot, peeled & chopped

3/4 cup dry, red wine

3/4 cup beef broth

2 cups crushed, canned tomatoes

6 tablespoons Parmigiano- Reggiano, finely grated

Pinch cayenne pepper

Sea salt & ground black pepper to taste

Directions

1. Insert the inner pot into the Power Cooker. Add oil and then set on RICE/RISOTTO mode. Add beef, stir and cook for 5 minutes.

2. Now add the onion, carrots and garlic and then keep cooking until the time expires.

3. Add the rest of the ingredients except the Parmigiano.

4. Cover and lock lid. Afterwards, switch the pressure release valve to closed. Press the button for WARM/CANCEL. Press the CHICKEN/MEAT button.

5. When the time expires, the cooker will automatically switch to KEEP WARM. Open pressure release. Wait for the steam is to completely released and then remove the lid.

6. Enjoy with Parmigiano-Reggiano.

Zesty Barbacoa Beef

Cumin, garlic, oregano, chipotle adobo and cloves are all combined in spicy shredded beef that is braised for your full pleasure.

Servings: 9

Preparation time: 15minutes

Cook time: 65 minutes

Ingredients:

3 lbs beef eye bottom or round roast, fat trimmed & cut into 3" pieces

5 cloves garlic

1 lime, juice

1/2 medium onion

2-4 tbsp chipotles in adobo sauce (to taste)

1 tablespoon ground oregano

1 cup water

1 tablespoon ground cumin + more

1/2 tsp ground cloves

2 1/2 teaspoons kosher salt

Black pepper

3 bay leaves

1 teaspoon oil

Directions:

1. In a blender, puree garlic, cumin, oregano, cloves, lime juice, chipotles, onion and water until smooth.

2. Season meat with 2 teaspoons of salt and black pepper. Place the inner pot inside the Power Cooker. Add oil and press the CHICKEN/MEAT button. Add the meat and brown for 5 minutes.

3. Add the pureed sauce and the bay leaves; cover and lock the Power Cooker and then and switch the pressure release valve to closed. Select WARM/CANCEL.

4. Press the SOUP/STEW STEW button and the Time button to 60 minutes. Once the timer gets to 0, the cooker will switch to Keep Warm automatically. .

5. Switch the pressure release valve to open to release the steam. Once all steam is released, remove the lid.

6. Transfer meat to a dish and shred with two forks, reserving the liquid for later but discarding the bay leaf.

7. Return the shredded beef to the Power Cooker; add 1 1/2 cups of the reserved liquid, 1/2 teaspoon of cumin and salt to taste. Serve and enjoy!

Tender Short Ribs

Servings: 8

Preparation time: 10 minutes

Cook time: 45 minutes

Ingredients:

8 short ribs, trimmed

8 red potatoes, small

2 cups beef stock

2 carrots, peeled& diced

2 stalks celery diced

1 medium onion, peeled & diced

3 cloves garlic, peeled &minced

2 tablespoons of tomato paste

2 tablespoons of olive oil

1 tablespoon of sea salt

1 t tablespoon of black pepper, freshly ground

1 sprig rosemary

1 sprig thyme

1 bay leaf

Directions

1. Rub salt and pepper over the short ribs to season. Pour the olive oil into the inner pot of the Power Cooker and press the CHICKEN/MEAT button. Add the ribs to the inner pot and brown on both sides.

2. Remove the ribs to a plate and set to one side. Add the garlic and veggies, select STEAM and the select button to 4 minutes before adding the paste.

3. Return ribs to pot, along with the remaining ingredients.

4. Cover and lock lid and then switch the pressure release valve to closed. Press the button for the WARM/CANCEL.

5. Press the button for the SOUP/STEW mode and then adjust time to 40 Minutes.

6 Once the timer gets to 0, the cooker will switch to Keep Warm mode by itself.

7. Switch the pressure release valve to open in order to release the steam. Remove the lid when the steam is fully released. Serve!

Beef And Potato Stew (Carne Con Papas)

A quick-cooking classic Cuban beef stew and a family favorite.

Servings: 4

Preparation time: 10 minutes

Cook time: 20 minutes

Ingredients:

4 medium potatoes, peeled & largely diced

1 pound beef, cubed

½ white onions, largely diced

¼ green pepper, diced

3 clove garlic minced

½ teaspoon cumin

1 tablespoon oregano

8 oz tomato sauce

8 oz tomato, diced

6 oz dry white wine

1   bay leaf

2 oz vegetable oil

Salt & pepper to taste

4 oz water

Directions

1. Add oil to the inner pot of the Pressure Cooker. Press the CHICKEN/MEAT button and then sauté until well- browned. Remove and set beef to one side.

2. Sauté the onion, garlic and pepper, cooking until translucent. Add half of the white wine. Add the rest of the ingredients: cumin, tomato sauce, oregano, diced tomato, water, potatoes, bay leaf, and beef. Mix well.

3. Cover lid and lock, switch the pressure release valve to closed and then select WARM/CANCEL. Press the SOUP/STEW button and adjust time to 20 minutes.

4. Once the timer gets to 0, the cooker will switch to KEEP WARM automatically. Press the CANCEL button.

5. Turn the pressure release valve to open. Once the steam is completely released, remove the lid.

6. Serve with white rice.

POULTRY MAIN DISHES

Chili –Ginger Chicken

Serve these chicken thighs and sauce with rice, topped with either coleslaw on a hamburger bun, or coleslaw rolled into flour tortillas with romaine leaves.

Servings: 6

Preparation time: 4 hours 10 minutes

Cook time: 10 minutes

Ingredients:

3 pounds boneless, skinless chicken thighs

1 cup plain yogurt

2 teaspoons fresh ginger, grated

1 clove garlic, peeled & minced

¼ teaspoon cayenne pepper

4 tablespoons butter

8 teaspoons ketchup

1 14½-ounce can diced tomatoes

½ teaspoon chili powder

½ cup cashews, crushed

Salt& freshly ground black pepper, to taste

1 teaspoon sugar

Plain yogurt or sour cream, optional

2-3 drops red coloring, optional

Directions

1. Combine the yogurt, cayenne pepper, ginger and garlic in a bowl. Add chicken thighs and marinate for at least 4 hours; remove.

2. Insert the inner pot into the Power Cooker. Add the chicken thighs from marinade to it, together with the chili powder, ketchup and diced tomatoes.

3. Cover and lock lid and then turn the pressure release valve to closed. Press the SOUP/STEW button.

4. Once the timer gets to 0, the cooker will switch to Keep Warm mode by itself.

5. Switch the pressure release valve to open in order to release the steam. Remove the lid when the steam is fully released.

6. Puree the tomatoes with an immersion blender. Whisk in the sugar and butter. Add the cashews and stir. Add salt and pepper, to taste.

7. If you prefer your sauce less spicy, stir in some sour cream or plain yogurt 1 tablespoon at a time until desired taste is attained.

8. If desired, add red food coloring. Pour over the chicken thighs and serve.

Chicken Bordeaux

Serve with cooked rice, buttered egg noodles or potatoes.

Servings: 6

Preparation time: 10 minutes

Cook time: 20 minutes

Ingredients:

4 ounces mushrooms, sliced

3 pounds chicken pieces

1 14½-oz can diced tomatoes

3 tbsp vegetable oil

1 teaspoon cracked black pepper

1 clove garlic, peeled and crushed

1 cup dry white wine

Directions:

1. Season the chicken with pepper.

2. Put the inner pot into the Power Cooker and add oil and garlic to it and then sauté for a few minutes; discard the garlic.

3. Place the chicken pieces skin side down in the pot. Pour in the tomatoes and wine. Add the mushrooms. Press the button for WARM/CANCEL. Cover and lock the Power Cooker and then switch the pressure release valve to closed.

4. Press the SOUP/STEW Button. Once the timer gets to 0, the cooker will switch to Keep Warm.

5. Switch the pressure release valve to open. When the steam is completely released, remove the lid. Transfer chicken to a serving platter.

6. Lock lid of Power Cooker and switch the pressure release valve to closed. Select SOUP/STEW to thicken for 5 minutes.

7. Pour thickened sauce over the chicken on a platter. Serve!

Pressure Cooked Fall- Of- The- Bone Chicken

Servings: 10

Preparation time: 10 minutes

Cook time: 35 minutes

Ingredients:

1 whole 4lb chicken

1 teaspoon paprika

2 tablespoons lemon juice

1 tablespoon coconut oil

6 cloves garlic

1 teaspoon thyme, dried

½ teaspoon sea salt

11/2 chicken bone broth

¼ teaspoon of black pepper, freshly ground

Directions

1. Combine thyme, paprika, pepper, salt and thyme in a small bowl. Coat the chicken with the seasoning.

2. Add oil to the inner pot of the Power Cooker. Add chicken with the skin side down and select CHICKEN/MEAT for 5minutes.

3. Turn over chicken and then add lemon juice, garlic cloves and broth.

4. Cover and lock the Power Cooker, and then switch the pressure release valve to closed.

5. Set to WARM/CANCEL. Choose SOUP/STEW and adjust time to 20 minutes.

7. Once the time is up, turn the pressure release valve to open. Wait until the steam is totally released before opening the cover.

8. Remove chicken and set aside for 5 minutes. Cut and enjoy!

Asian Chicken & Rice

Servings: 4

Preparation time: 10 minutes

Cook time: 10 minutes

Ingredients:

2 chicken breasts, boneless & skinless, largely cut

1 green pepper, seeded and diced

1 clove garlic, peeled & minced

1 onion peeled & diced

1 tsp. ginger, minced

2 tbsp. grape- seed oil

3 scallions chopped

1 cup yellow white rice

1 bag frozen mixed vegetables

1 3/4 cup chicken stock

1 cup broccoli florets

Sea salt, to taste

Freshly ground black pepper, to taste

Directions

1. Rub salt and pepper all over chicken.

2. Add oil to the inner pot of the Power Cooker. Press the CHICKEN/MEAT button and sauté the chicken and veggies.

3. Add the rice, stir and then add the remaining ingredients.

4. Cover, lock lid and turn the pressure release valve to closed. Select WARM/CANCEL and then the RICE/RISSOTO option.

5. Once the timer reaches 0, the Power Cooker will automatically go to KEEP WARM. Turn the pressure release valve to open. Remove lid once the steam is completely released.

6. *Serve!*

Sunday Chicken & Dressing
Servings: 4

Preparation time: 10 minutes

Cook time: 6 minutes

Ingredients

1 stalk celery, chopped

2 to 2-1/2 pounds bone-in chicken pieces

1 tablespoon margarine or butter

1 teaspoon paprika

1/2 cup chopped onion

1 teaspoon rubbed sage

4 cups herb-seasoned stuffing

2 tablespoons minced fresh parsley

1 teaspoon salt

1/2 teaspoon pepper

1 cup water

1/2 cup sliced mushrooms, optional

Directions

1. Sprinkle the chicken with paprika.

2. Add butter to the inner pot of the Power Cooker. Melt, using the CHICKEN/MEAT button and then add chicken in small quantities and brown on both sides evenly. Set browned chicken aside.

3. Stir celery, mushroom and onion into the melted butter. Cook again for 3 minutes and then add the sage, parsley, salt and pepper into the vegetables, stirring well.

4. Place the chicken over vegetables and add water.

5. Cover and lock lid and turn the pressure release valve to closed. Press the button for the WARM/CANCEL mode.

6. Select SOUP/STEW and adjust time to 20 minutes. Once the timer gets to 0, the Power Cooker will switch to Keep Warm mode.

7. Switch the pressure release valve to open in order to release the steam. Remove the lid when the steam is fully released.

8. Lift chicken out of liquid using a slotted spoon, leaving vegetables and liquid in pot.

9. Set chicken. Add the stuffing into liquid and stir. Cover and lock lid, switching the pressure release valve to close. Press the FISH/VEG/STEAM button.

10. Serve the dressing with chicken.

Spicy Chicken Salad

If the chicken is prepared the night before and refrigerated in its own broth, the chicken will be very moist.

Servings: 6

Preparation time: 15 minutes

Cook time: 10 minutes

Ingredients

1 medium sweet onion, peeled &quartered

3 pounds chicken breast halves, bone-in and with skin

1 stalk celery, diced

1 large carrot, peeled & diced

8 peppercorns

1½ cups apples, diced

½ cup sour cream

1 cup slivered almonds, toasted

2 tablespoons red onion or shallot, diced

¼ cup mayonnaise

½ cup seedless green grapes, halved

1 cup celery, sliced

2–3 tablespoons curry powder

½ teaspoon of freshly ground black pepper

Salt, to taste

1 cup water

Directions

1. Add the chicken, peppercorns, onion, celery, carrot and water to the inner pot of the Power Cooker.

2. Close lid and lock it. Switch the pressure release valve to closed. Select SOUP/STEW.

3. Once the cooker automatically switches to KEEP WARM, turn the pressure release valve to open to fully release steam. Remove the lid.

4. With a slotted spoon, transfer chicken to bowl. Strain the broth that is in the pot and then pour it over the chicken. Leave the chicken in the broth to cool.

5. To make the salad, add the curry powder, sour cream, mayonnaise, pepper and salt pepper to a bowl. Stir well. Add the almonds, celery, apples, and shallot or red onion.

6. Remove chicken from the bones. Throw away the bones and skin. Now dice the chicken and fold them into the salad mixture. Refrigerate until ready to serve.

Balsamic Chicken & Onions
Servings: 2

Preparation time: 5 minutes

Cook time: 20 minutes

Ingredients

1½ lb Chicken Thighs

2 chicken cubes

2 cups of sweet onions, minced

2 cups carrots, chopped

1 cup raisins or mixed berries

6 garlic cloves or more

1 cup balsamic vinegar

2 bay leaves

1 cup red wine

Directions

1. Insert the inner pot into the Power Cooker and then put all the ingredients in it. Add salt and pepper if you like.

2. Close and lock the lid then switch the pressure release valve to closed. Select SOUP/STEW and adjust time to 20 minutes.

3. Once the timer gets to 0, the cooker will switch to Keep Warm automatically. Switch the pressure release valve to open to release the steam. Remove the lid when steam is fully released.

4. Enjoy with rice and mashed potatoes.

Buffalo Chicken Wings
Servings: 4

Preparation time: 0 minutes

Cook time: 10 minutes

Ingredients

4 lbs frozen chicken wings

3/4 cup Hot Sauce

Butter

Directions

1. Pour the sauce into the inner pot of the Power Cooker. Add a little butter and mix to blend well.

2. Coat the wings with the mixed sauce.

3. Place the lid on, lock it and switch the pressure release valve to closed. Select SOUP/STEW.

4. Once the timer gets to 0, the cooker will switch to KEEP WARM. Open pressure release valve to release steam and then remove the lid.

5. Serve with dressing of choice.

Chicken &Tomatillo Sauce
Enjoy this mild but savory dish.

Servings: 4

Preparation time: 10 minutes

Cook time: 15 minutes

Ingredients:

1-2 tablespoon of olive oil

1 large onion, sliced

1 teaspoon garlic powder or 1 clove garlic, crushed

2lb boneless/skinless chicken thighs

14 oz tomatillos or salsa verde

1 can green chilies

Salt and pepper, to taste

1 tsp ground coriander or1 handful fresh cilantro

¾ cups garbanzo beans

3 cups cheddar cheese

1 ¾ cups of leftover rice

½ cup black olives

¾ cups chopped tomatoes

Directions

1. In your Power Cooker, sauté onions in oil, using the CHICKEN/MEAT mode until translucent. Add garlic and sauté for 15 seconds and then add the chicken, chilies, cilantro, tomatillos, salt and pepper to taste.

2. Place the lid on, lock it and switch the pressure release valve to closed. Afterwards, press the button for the WARM/CANCEL setting.

3. Select SOUP/STEW. Once the timer gets to 0, the cooker will switch to Keep Warm on its own.

4. Switch the pressure release valve to open so as to release the steam. Once all steam is released, remove the lid.

5. Remove the chicken and break it up with two forks. Add rice and garbanzo beans. Cover and close pressure valve.

6. Select STEAM. When the program ends, open valve and release steam.

7. Put the meat back to the pot to reheat. Add the cheese and stir.

8. Serve with refried beans salad and tortillas. It can be used as a burrito filling as well.

Duck And Veggies

After a hard day's work, you will enjoy this delicious duck cooked with vegetables.

Servings: 8

Preparation time: 15 minutes

Cook time: 30 minutes

Ingredients:

1 cucumber cut into pieces

1 medium size duck

2 carrots cut into pieces

2 tablespoons wine or 1 tablespoon cooking wine

1 small ginger, cut into pieces

2 teaspoons of salt

2 cups of water

Directions

1. Place the inner pot into the Power Cooker. Add all ingredients

2. Cover and lock lid and then turn the pressure release valve to closed. Press the SOUP/STEW button.

3. Once the timer gets to 0, the cooker will switch to Keep Warm mode.

4. Switch the pressure release valve to open in order to release the steam. Remove the lid when the steam is fully released.

5. Serve and enjoy.

Steamed Chicken With Traditional Chinese Garlic Sauce

A well- loved popular traditional Chinese dish.

Servings: 6

Preparation time: 30 minutes

Cook time: 12 minutes

Ingredients:

9 pieces Chicken drumsticks (about 2 .2lb)

1 tablespoon olive oil

2 tablespoon freshly minced garlic

1 tablespoon Chinese salted fermented soya beans (minced &black colored)

1 tablespoon green onion, freshly chopped

For Marinade

1 tablespoon Kikkoman light soy sauce

1 tablespoon dark soy sauce

2/3 teaspoon salt

11/2 tablespoon corn starch

2 tablespoon water

Directions

1. Begin by cleaning the chicken drumsticks, removing the bones and then cutting them into pieces. Mix all the marinade ingredients together, add drumsticks. Refrigerate overnight in a lidded container.

2. Insert the inner pot into the Power Cooker. Add the olive oil and the minced Chinese salted fermented soya beans and garlic. Select STEAM and then transfer to a bowl. Now mix thoroughly with the marinated chicken.

3. Pour 2 cups water in the pot, place the steamer tray and then place the bowl with the chicken on it.

4. Close and lock the lid then switch the pressure release valve to closed. Press the WARM/CANCEL button. Select SOUP/STEW.

5. Once the timer gets to 0, the cooker will switch to Keep Warm automatically. Switch the pressure release valve to open to release the steam. Remove the lid when steam is fully released.

6. Remove the bowl. Add green onion, mix and serve

Power Cooked Turkey Chili
A delicious chili you can't resist!

Servings: 4

Preparation time: minutes

Cook time: 10 minutes

Ingredients:

1 lb lean ground turkey

15 oz chick peas (previously cooked)

1 yellow bell pepper, diced

I medium onion, diced

2 – 3 cloves garlic, peeled

21/2 tablespoons of chili powder

11/2 teaspoon cumin

1/8 teaspoon cayenne

2 cans original rotel

4-5 ounces water

1 –5.5 ounces can V8

12-ounces vegetable stock or12 ounces water with vegetable stock

Directions

1. Insert the inner pot into the Power Cooker. Add the ground turkey and water to it.

2. Close and lock the lid then switch the pressure release valve to closed. Select BEANS/ LENTILS (5mins).

3. Switch the pressure release valve to open to release the steam. Remove the lid when steam is released completely.

4. Break up the ground turkey and add the rest of the ingredients to your Power Cooker. Press the WARM/CANCEL button. Select BEANS/ LENTILS (5mins)

5. Serve and enjoy!

Braised Turkey Thighs In The Power Cooker

The low-temperature setting can also be used for this yummy turkey dish. Simply set your Power Cooker to slow cook for 4 hours.

Servings: 4

Preparation time: 10 minutes

Cook time: 1 hour: 15 minutes

Ingredients:

2 turkey thighs (about 1 lb), trimmed of excess fat

1 cup chicken broth

1 tbsp red-wine vinegar

1 cup onions, thinly sliced

1 cup Portobello mushrooms, sliced

2 tsp minced garlic

½ tsp dried rosemary

½ tsp thyme

½ tsp sage

½ tsp salt and pepper

Gravy:

¼ cup water

3 tbsp flour

Directions

1. Place the inner pot into the Power Cooker. Select CHICKEN/MEAT and brown turkey thighs. Add all other ingredients.

2. Close and lock the lid then turn the pressure release valve to closed. Select WARM/CANCEL, and then SOUP/STEW, adjusting time to 60 minutes.

3. Switch the pressure release valve to open so as to release the steam. Once all steam is released, remove the lid.

4. Once meat is done, remove to cutting board and cover with foil.

5. To make gravy, whisk flour and water in a small bowl until thoroughly blended. Add the flour mixture into the onions, liquid and mushrooms in the Power Cooker, mixing well.

6. Close and lock the lid then turn the pressure release valve to closed. Press the WARM/CANCEL button. Select CHICKEN/MEAT (15mins).

7. Once the timer gets to 0, the cooker will switch to Keep Warm automatically. Switch the pressure release valve to open to release the steam. Remove the lid when steam is fully released.

8. Arrange on 4 serving plates and spoon on some gravy.

Romano Chicken

Servings: 4

Preparation time: 5 minutes

Cook time: 15 minutes

Ingredients:

1 tablespoon of all-purpose flour

1 onion minced

½ teaspoon salt

½ teaspoon pepper

6 boneless skinless chicken, cut into chunks

2 tbsp oil

1 (10-ounce) can tomato sauce

1 (4-ounce can) sliced mushrooms

1 teaspoon vinegar

1 tbsp sugar

1 tbsp dried oregano

1 teaspoon dried basil

1 teaspoon chicken bouillon granules

1 cup Romano cheese

1 teaspoon garlic – minced

1 tbsp butter, at room temperature

Directions

1. In your Power Cooker inner pot, Sauté chicken in oil until brown using the CHICKEN/MEAT setting. Add onion and garlic and sauté until translucent. Add the remaining ingredients except the flour, butter and Romano cheese and stir to combine.

2. Close and lock the lid then turn the pressure release valve to closed. Press the WARM/CANCEL button. Select SOUP/STEW (10mins).

3. Once the time expires, the cooker will switch to Keep Warm automatically. Switch the pressure release valve to open to release the steam. Remove the lid when steam is fully released.

4. Add the Romano cheese and stir. Thicken sauce by adding a mixture of butter and flour. Add this paste to the cooked sauce to thicken it.

5. Serve over rice or pasta or enjoy alone.

PORK MAIN DISHES

Pork Loin Dinner

Serve this delicious dinner with a tossed salad and warm buttered dinner rolls.

Servings: 4

Preparation time: 15 minutes

Cook time: 27 minutes

Ingredients:

1 pound pork loin, boneless

4 small Yukon Gold or red potatoes, scrubbed, cut into quarters

1 small onion, peeled & diced

1 tablespoon vegetable oil

½ cup apple juice or white wine

1 cup chicken broth

1 large turnip, peeled & diced

1 rutabaga, peeled & diced

½ teaspoon mild curry powder

1 stalk celery, finely diced

¼ teaspoon dried thyme

4 carrots, peeled and diced

½ cup sliced leeks, white part only

2 teaspoons dried parsley

3 tablespoons fresh lemon juice

2 tart green or Granny Smith apples, peeled, cored& diced

Salt and freshly ground black pepper, to taste

Fresh parsley or thyme sprigs, optional

Directions:

1. Add oil to inner pot of Power Cooker. Add the onion and sauté for 3 minutes. Add the pork and season lightly with salt and pepper. Press CHICKEN/MEAT and cook for 5 minutes.

2. Add the apple juice or wine, broth, turnip and rutabaga. Add the potatoes to the pot along with the celery, carrots, curry powder, leeks, parsley, lemon juice and thyme.

3. Place lid on pot, secure and then switch the pressure release valve to closed. Select CANCEL. Select CHICKEN/MEAT again. Once the timer gets to 0, the cooker will immediately switch to KEEP WARM.

4. Switch the pressure release valve to open. When steam is completely released, open the lid and add the diced apples. Lock lid. Press STEAM and adjust time to 4 minutes.

5. Wait for steam to release fully and then serve, garnished with thyme or fresh parsley.

Braised Pork Ribs In Soy Sauce

Servings: 6

Preparation time: 5 minutes

Cook time: 40 minutes

Ingredients:

2 lb spareribs

1 tbsp olive oil

3-4 fresh ginger, sliced

1 green onion, rinsed & cut into 2 inches length

1 star anise

2 cloves

11/2 tbsp anka sauce or 11/2 tsp red yeast rice

1 tbsp cooking wine

11/2 tablespoons premium dark soy sauce

1 tablespoon light soy sauce

1 tablespoon premium light soy sauce

1/2 tsp salt

1 1/2 tablespoons honey

4 tbsp water

Directions:

1. Wash ribs with warm water and cut into small pieces. Soak 2 minutes in boiling water. Drain, rinse and drain again.

2. Add oil to Power Cooker, select the CHICKEN/MEAT option and add ginger, green onion, cloves and anise and sauté 1 minute. Add red yeast rice or anka sauce and ribs, stir and cook 2 minutes.

3. Add cooking wine and stir occasionally. Add cooking wine, premium dark soy sauce, light soy sauce, salt, honey and water.

4. Place lid on, lock and switch pressure release valve to closed. Select WARM/CANCEL. Set it on SOUP/STEW mode and time to 30 Minutes. Once the timer gets to 0, the cooker will switch to KEEP WARM.

5. Turn the pressure release valve to open. Remove lid once the steam is fully released.

6. Select SOUP/STEW on your Power Cooker; stir a few times until the sauce reduces to 1/4.

7. Place the cooked pork into to a bowl and serve over rice.

Braised Ribs With Spirulina And Woodears

Get your dried spirulina and woodears from the Chinese grocery store nearest to you and prepare this awesomely tasty dinner dish.

Servings: 6

Preparation time: 15 minutes

Cook time: 30 minutes

Ingredients:

1½ lb baby back ribs, membranes removed

5 small dried Chinese mushrooms

¼ oz dried black Chinese fungus (black woodears)

½ oz dried spirulina

1½ tbsp olive oil

2 green onions washed and chopped to 1 inch long

2-3 slices of ginger

1 anise star

2 cloves

1 tbsp cooking wine

3/4 tsp salt

1 ½ tsp sugar

1½ tbsp light soy sauce

1½ tbsp premium soy sauce

1½ tbsp dark soy sauce

Directions:

1. Soak the dried mushrooms and the black fungus in cold water for 2-4hours, rinse and drain. Soak dried spirulina in cold water for 1 hour, rinse and drain and then set aside. Wash ribs, cut into pieces, rinse and drain.

2. Place the inner pot into the Power Cooker. Add oil, sliced ginger, chopped green onion, cloves and anise star. Set on CHICKEN/MEAT and cook for 30 seconds.

3. Add the pork ribs; cook 3-4 minutes until slightly brown outside. Add cooking wine, the premium soy sauce, dark soy sauce, light soy sauce, salt, sugar, black fungus and mushrooms.

4. Cover and lock, and then turn the pressure release valve to closed. Press the button for the WARM/CANCEL.

5. Set it on RICE/RISOTTO mode and select time button to 18 Minutes. Once the timer gets to 0, the cooker will switch to KEEP WARM.

6. Turn the pressure release valve to open. Remove lid once the steam is fully released. Add the spirulina. Cover the lid, place pressure valve to closed and press STEAM (2 min).

7. When the program is done, release the pressure and open the lid. Remove to a serving bowl and serve with steamed rice.

Flavorful Pork Roast

Servings: 8- 10

Preparation time: 20 minutes

Cook time: 55 minutes

Ingredients:

1 tbsp vegetable oil

1 3-pound boneless pork loin

5 cloves minced garlic

1 cup white wine or water

1 tbsp lemon juice

1 tbsp chopped fresh rosemary

1 tsp grated lemon zest

1/2 tsp dried thyme leaves

1 tbsp olive oil

1/2 cup water

1/2 tsp salt

1/4 tsp pepper

Directions

1. Add oil to the inner pot of the Power Cooker. Press CHICKEN/MEAT. Add pork roast and brown the meat on all sides evenly.

2. Meanwhile, place rosemary, garlic, thyme, lemon zest, salt, pepper, olive oil and lemon juice in a small bowl, mixing well.

3. Remove the browned pork roast from the cooker and set aside. Place the tray in the cooker and water and wine.

4. Place the browned pork roast on tray. With a pastry brush, brush sides and top of roast with the rosemary mixture.

5. Cover and lock, and then turn the pressure release valve to closed. Press the button for the WARM/CANCEL.

6. Set it on SOUP/STEW mode and adjust time to 50 Minutes. Once the timer gets to 0, the cooker will switch to KEEP WARM.

7. Switch the pressure release valve to open in order to release the steam. Remove the lid when the steam is fully released.

Classic Cassoulet

Cook this classic provincial French dish within an hour!

Servings: 4-6

Preparation time: 10 minutes

Cook time: 45 minutes

Ingredients:

2 pounds pork ribs, boneless cut into chunks of 1-inch

1 cup beef broth

4 cloves garlic, minced

2 cups of great Northern beans

2 tablespoons olive oil

2 cups herbed croutons

1 carrot, diced

1 celery stalk, diced

½ white onion, diced

2 tablespoons dried rosemary

Salt& fresh pepper to taste

1 cup goat cheese, crumbled, optional

Directions

1. Sprinkle the pork ribs with salt and pepper.

2. Place the inner pot in the power Cooker. Select CHICKEN/MEAT and then brown on all sides.

3. Add the beans, carrot, broth, celery, rosemary, onion and garlic.

4. Lock lid into place and switch the pressure release valve to closed. Select WARM/CANCEL. Set it on BEANS/ LENTILS mode and select time to 30 Minutes. Once the timer gets to 0, the cooker will switch to KEEP WARM.

5. Turn the pressure release valve to open. Remove lid once the steam is fully released.

6. Ladle into large soup bowls, top with croutons and goat cheese.

Fruit Sauced Pork Steak

Serve over mashed potatoes and some steam-in-the-bag green beans.

Servings: 6

Preparation time: 10 minutes

Cook time: 20 minutes

Ingredients

8 pitted prunes

71

4 8-ounce pork steaks, trimmed of fat

2 small Granny Smith apples, peeled, cored& sliced

½ cup heavy cream

½ cup dry white wine or apple juice

1 tablespoon red currant jelly

1 tablespoon butter, optional

Salt and freshly ground pepper, to taste

Directions

1. Add the pork steaks, prunes, apple slices, cream and apple juice or wine to the inner pot of the Power Cooker. Add salt and pepper to taste.

2. Cover and lock, and then turn the pressure release valve to closed. Set it on SOUP/ STEW mode (10mins). Once the timer gets to 0, the cooker will switch to keep warm automatically.

3. Switch the pressure release valve to open in order to release the steam. Remove the lid when the steam is fully released.

4. Transfer meat and fruit to a platter. Simmer uncovered for 10 minutes.

5. Once mixture reduces by half and thickens, whisk in the red currant jelly. Add more salt and pepper if necessary. If you prefer a richer, glossier sauce, whisk in the butter 1teaspoon at a time.

Slow- Cooked Pulled Pork

Servings: 4

Preparation time: 10 minutes

Cook time: 10 hours

Ingredients

4 lbs boneless pork picnic shoulder or pork butt

1 medium onion, peeled & finely chopped

Kosher salt

12 oz smoky BBQ sauce

1 teaspoon cumin

1 teaspoon coriander

1/2 teaspoon cayenne pepper

3 cups water

Soft hamburger rolls

Directions

1. Place the inner pot in the Power Cooker. Put in all the ingredients except Hamburger rolls and BBQ Sauce.

2. Cover, lock the lid and turn the pressure release valve to closed.

3. Press the SLOW COOK button and adjust time to 10 hours.

4. Once the timer gets to 0, the cooker will switch to KEEP WARM. Turn the pressure release valve to open. Remove lid once the steam is fully released.

 5. Remove the pork, shred, and add the BBQ sauce. Serve and enjoy on soft hamburger rolls.

German Pork Chops & Sauerkraut

Servings: 4

Preparation time: 10 minutes

Cook time: 10 minutes

Ingredients:

1 1-pound bag baby carrots

1 stalk celery, finely chopped

1 large onion, peeled & sliced

1 12-ounce can beer

4 slices bacon, cut into small pieces

1 clove garlic, peeled & minced

4 1-inch-thick bone-in pork loin chops

4 medium red potatoes, peeled & quartered

1 1-pound bag sauerkraut, rinsed & drained

2 teaspoons Bavarian seasoning

Salt & freshly ground pepper, to taste

Directions

1. Place the Inner Pot in the Power Cooker.

2. To it, add the stalk, carrot, onion, garlic, bacon, pork loin chops, sauerkraut, potatoes, beer, Bavarian seasoning, salt and pepper.

3. Place lid and lock; switch the pressure release valve to closed. Press the button for SOUP/STEW (10mins). Once the timer gets to 0, the cooker will switch to KEEP WARM automatically.

4. Switch the pressure release valve to open in order to release the steam. Remove the lid when the steam is fully released.

5. If necessary, add more seasoning. Serve hot.

Kielbasa, Kraut & Cabbage

Servings: 4

Preparation time: 5 minutes

Cook time: 10 minutes

Ingredients:

1 pound smoked, well cooked sausage or Kielbasa, cut into 2-inch pieces

1 can (16 oz) sauerkraut, drained

1 bacon, sliced, cut into 1/2-inch pieces

3 cups shredded green cabbage

1 onion, chopped

1 tablespoon brown sugar

1/4 teaspoon celery seed

1 cup water

1 teaspoon salt

1/4 teaspoon pepper

Directions

1. Place the bacon in the inner pot of the Power Cooker. Press the CHICKEN/MEAT button and brown for 3 minutes.

2. Add onion and cook for 3 or 4 minutes. Add remaining ingredients.

3. Cover and lock the Power Cooker, and then switch the pressure release valve to closed. Press the WARM/CANCEL button.

4. Press the button for BEANS/LENTIL (5mins).

5. Once the timer gets to 0, the cooker will switch to Keep Warm by itself.

6. Switch the pressure release valve to open in order to release the steam. Remove the lid when the steam is fully released.

BBQ Western Ribs

For a delicious, casual meal, add potato chips and coleslaw.

Servings: 4

Preparation time: 15minutes

Cook time: 60 minutes

Ingredients:

1 3-inch cinnamon stick

3 pounds pork Western ribs

1 cup barbeque sauce

6 whole cloves

½ cup apple jelly

½ cup water

1 large sweet onion, peeled & diced

Directions

1. Add the cinnamon stick, barbeque sauce, cloves, water, onion and jelly to the inner pot of the Power Cooker and stir.

2. Add the ribs, spooning some sauce over them.

3. Cover and lock the lid of the Power Cooker and turn the pressure release valve to closed. Press the button for Soup/STEW and adjust time to 50 minutes. Once the timer gets to 0, the cooker will switch to KEEP WARM automatically.

4. Switch the pressure release valve to open in order to release the steam. Remove the lid when the steam is fully released.

5. Remove the bones and meat; cover and keep warm. Skim fat from sauce. Remove cloves and cinnamon stick and return to pot.

6. Cook uncovered, at medium-high temperature, until the sauce is lessened and coats the back of a spoon.

7. (To stretch this recipe to 8 servings, serve barbeque pork sandwiches rather than 4 servings of pork).

Easy Green Chili
Servings: 2

Preparation time: 5 minutes

Cook time: 20 minutes

Ingredients:

1 pound of pork

1 cup green salsa

Directions:

1. Cut the pork into sizes of stew meat and add to the inner pot of Power Cooker. Set on CHICKEN/MEAT mode until brown. Pour the salsa over it.

2. Cover and lock the lid of the Power Cooker and switch the pressure release valve to closed. Select CANCEL.

3. Press the button for SOUP/STEW and then adjust time to 20 minutes. Once the timer gets to 0, the cooker will switch to KEEP WARM automatically.

4. Switch the pressure release valve to open in order to release the steam. Remove the lid when the steam is fully released.

5. Serve and enjoy!

Braised Pork Ribs With Bamboo Shoots And Garlic
This great- tasting dish goes well with steamed rice.

Servings: 6

Preparation time: 10 minutes

Cook time: 45 minutes

Ingredients:

2lb spare ribs, membrane removed

¼ cup winter shoots, dried

1 tablespoon of olive oil

2-3 fresh ginger, sliced

2 green onion rinsed & cut into 2-inch length

5-6 garlic cloves

1 star anise

1 tablespoon cooking wine

2 tablespoon premium dark soy sauce

11/2 tbsp light soy sauce

1/2 tsp salt

3 tbsp water

½ teaspoon of sugar

1 teaspoon of sesame oil

Directions:

1. Soak the dried bamboo shoots in cold water for 8 straight hours. Rinse and drain. Wash ribs and cut them into small pieces between bones; rinse and drain.

2. Sauté the green onion, star anise, ginger and garlic for 1-2 minutes in your Power Cooker. Add the pork ribs; Select CHICKEN/MEAT and cook for 3 to 4 minutes until just brown.

3. Add bamboo shoots, cooking for 1-2 more minutes. Now, add coking wine, premium dark soy sauce, light soy sauce, salt, sugar and water and bring to a boil.

4. Secure lid on the Power Cooker, and then switch the pressure release valve to closed. Press the WARM/CANCEL setting. Select SOUP/ STEW and adjust time to 30minutes. When done, the Power Cooker will switch to KEEP WARM automatically.

5. Turn the pressure release valve to open. Wait until the steam is released completely before opening the cover.

6. Cook and stir every now and then until the sauce is reduced to a quarter.

7. Transfer to a bowl. Serve over rice and enjoy.

Almost Sweet Pork

Serve over Chinese noodles or cooked. Place soy sauce and toasted sesame oil at the table.

Servings: 8

Preparation time: 15 minutes

Cook time: 30 minutes

Ingredients:

1 tablespoon all-purpose flour

2 pounds pork shoulder, cut into bite-size pieces

1 14-ounce can pineapple chunks

2 tablespoons peanut or sesame oil

1/8 teaspoon mustard powder

1 tablespoon light brown sugar

½ teaspoon ground ginger

1 tablespoon low-sodium soy sauce

2 tablespoons apple cider vinegar

1 large red bell pepper, seeded & sliced

4 medium carrots, peeled & sliced

½ pound fresh sugar snap peas

2 cloves garlic, peeled & thinly sliced

2 cups fresh broccoli florets, cut into bite-size pieces

2 large sweet onions, peeled & diced

2 tablespoons cornstarch

1 cup bean sprouts

2 tablespoons cold water

Directions

1. Add the pork pieces to a zip-closure bag and add the flour; seal and shake to coat the pork.

2. Add oil to the Power Cooker and brown pork for 3 minutes on CHICKEN/MEAT mode. Add the pineapple juice (reserve the pineapple chunks); mix well.

3. Add the mustard powder, sugar, vinegar, ginger, carrots, Liquid Aminos or soy sauce, sugar snap peas and red bell pepper. Add the broccoli florets, ¾ onion and garlic.

4. Cover and lock, and then turn the pressure release valve to closed. Select CANCEL. Set it on CHICKEN/MEAT (15mins). Once the timer gets to 0, the cooker will switch to KEEP WARM.

5. Turn the pressure release valve to open. Remove lid once the steam is fully released

6. With a slotted spoon, transfer all the solids to a serving platter; keep warm.

7. To make the glaze, combine the cornstarch and water in a small bowl. Add some of the pan juices and stir.

8. Add to the Power Cooker, and stir in the cornstarch mixture. Lock lid and close pressure release valve. Select BEANS/LENTILS (5 min).

9. Once the timer gets to 0, the cooker will switch to KEEP WARM. Turn the pressure release valve to open. Remove lid once the steam is fully released

10. Add the bean sprouts, onion and reserved pineapple chunks and stir. Pour over the vegetables and cooked pork in the serving platter; stir to mix. Enjoy!

Balsamic Pork Chops& Figs

Serve with a tossed salad, baked potatoes, steamed vegetable and top with toasted walnuts and diced apples.

Servings: 4

Preparation time: 15 minutes

Cook time: 35 minutes

Ingredients

½ cup chicken broth

10 ounces dried figs

4 1-inch-thick bone-in pork loin chops

2 teaspoons ghee or butter

2 medium sweet onions, peeled & sliced

2 teaspoons extra virgin olive oil

4 cloves garlic, peeled & minced

3 tablespoons balsamic vinegar

½ teaspoon dried thyme

2 tablespoons dry white wine

Salt & freshly ground black pepper, to taste

Directions

1. Season the pork chops lightly on both sides by sprinkling with salt & pepper. Add the oil and ghee or butter to the inner pot of the power Cooker. Add pork chops and brown on the CHICKEN/MEAT mode. Transfer chops to a platter.

2. Add the onions; sautéing for 4 minutes then stir in the garlic and sauté for 30 seconds. Stir in the balsamic vinegar and thyme. Cook uncovered until vinegar is lessened by half.

4. Stir in the broth and wine. Add the pork chops, spoon some onions over the chops and place the figs on top.

5. Cover and lock, and then turn the pressure release valve to closed. Press CANCEL. Select SOUP STEW (10mins) once the timer gets to 0, the cooker will switch to KEEP WARM.

6. Switch the pressure release valve to open so as to release the steam. Once all steam is released, remove the lid.

Make a Syrupy Sauce

1. Using a slotted spoon, transfer the onions, pork chops, and figs to a serving plate; cover and keep warm.

2. Simmer, uncovered in the pot until the pan juices are lessened.

3. Transfer the figs, onions and pork chops onto the serving platter.

Pork Hock With Agarics Mushrooms

This is a very scrumptious pork dish that even tastes better with rice.

Servings: 6

Preparation time: 20 minutes

Cook time: 40 minutes

Ingredients

2 lb boneless pork hock, cut into 1-inch cubes

20 agarics mushrooms, dry

1 anise star

1 green onion, chopped to 2-inch lengthwise

1 tablespoon olive oil

2 cloves

1 tsp fresh ginger, sliced

1 tablespoon cooking wine

1 tablespoon light soy sauce

1 teaspoon dark vinegar

1 teaspoon sugar

1 tablespoon dark soy sauce

1/2 teaspoon salt

Directions:

1. Soak the agarics mushrooms in cold water for 4-5 hours, rinse and set aside.

2. Place the pork inside the Inner Pot of your Power Cooker and fill it with boiling water, press the CHICKEN/MEAT button to brown, remove and rinse under cold water.

3. Add the olive oil, green onion, anise cloves and ginger to pot and sauté for a minute. Now add cooking wine and sauté 30 seconds. Return the pork hock meat to the Pot, and sauté 1 or 2 minutes. Add the soaked agarics mushrooms, mixing thoroughly.

4. Add dark vinegar, sugar, light soy sauce and dark soy sauce, mixing well. Secure lid and switch the pressure release valve to the closed position. Select WARM/CANCEL.

5. Select SOUP/STEW. Once the timer gets to 0, the cooker will switch to Keep Warm mode by itself.

6. Release the pressure then open the lid. Cook and stir until the sauce reduces to 1/3.

7. Remove the cooked meat to a serving dish and serve over rice.

Pressure Cooker Kakuni

Have a taste of Japan by trying this great-tasting Japanese recipe.

Servings: 3-4

Preparation time: 5 minutes

Cook time: 45 minutes

Ingredients

2 lb. pork belly block

3 green onions

1 tablespoon of vegetable oil

½ cup water

4 boiled eggs

½ cup soy sauce

¼ cup sake

½ cup mirin

1 inch ginger

¼ cup sugar

Japanese 7 spices (Shichimi Togarashi) for taste, optional

Water

Seasonings

Directions

1. Cut the green part of the onions in half. Peel and slice ginger thinly.

2. Press the CHICKEN/MEAT function on your Power Cooker, heat the oil and then cook the pork belly.

3. Pour water to cover the pork, add the green onions and ginger and secure lid. Switch the pressure release valve to closed. Select WARM/CANCEL.

4. Press the button for SOUP/STEW and select time to 30 minutes. Once the program ends, the cooker will switch to Keep Warm by itself. Turn the pressure release valve to open. Wait until the steam is released completely before opening the cover.

5. Drain the water and discard the ginger and green onion. Rinse the pork belly with warm water.

6. Return the meat to the cooker; add sake, mirin, ½ cup water, sugar and soy sauce. Mix the seasonings and add the boiled eggs. Simmer on high temperature to let the alcohol evaporate.

7. Once it evaporates, secure lid. Press the SOUP/STEW button (10mins).

8. Once done, release pressure, remove lid and simmer until the liquid has reduced by half.

9. Serve the pork belly, boiled egg and green vegetables, if any, over rice. To make it spicier, sprinkle Japanese 7 spices (shichimi toagarashi) over it.

SEAFOOD MAIN DISHES

Fish With Beer & Potato

With your Power Cooker, this delicious but challenging recipe for beginners is now easy to prepare.

Servings: 6

Preparation time: 15 minutes

Cook time: 40 minutes

Ingredients:

1 pound fish fillet

1 cup beer

1 tablespoon oyster flavored sauce

4 medium size potatoes, peeled and diced

1 tablespoon oil

1 red pepper sliced

1 tablespoon of rock candy

1 teaspoon salt

Directions

1. Place the inner pot into the Power Cooker and add in the ingredients.

2. Place the lid on, lock it and switch the pressure release valve to closed.

3. Choose FISH/ VEG/ STEAM. Once the timer gets to 0, the Power Cooker will switch to Keep Warm mode.

4. Switch the pressure release valve to open in order to release the steam. Remove the lid when the steam is fully released.

5. When the program is done, release the pressure by turning the pressure release valve to open then open the lid

6. Serve and enjoy.

Shrimp Chicken Jambalaya
Servings: 4-6

Preparation time: 10 minutes

Cook time: 10 minute

Ingredients

12 ounces large shrimp, peeled & deveined

2 skinless, boneless, chicken breast halves, cut into 1/2-inch cubes

1 cup converted rice, uncooked

1 onion, chopped

1 large green pepper, diced

3 stalks celery, sliced

2 cloves garlic, minced

1 can (8 ounces) tomato sauce

1 tablespoon vegetable oil

1-1/4 cups chicken broth

1/2 teaspoon dried thyme leaves

1/2 teaspoon salt

1 bay leaf

1/2 teaspoon white pepper

1/4 teaspoon cayenne pepper

2 dashes hot pepper sauce

1/2 teaspoon sage

Directions

1. Insert the inner pot in your Power Cooker. Add vegetable oil into it. Set it to CHICKEN/MEAT mode and let it heat. Afterwards, add onion, chicken, garlic green pepper and celery, sautéing until just tender.

2. Add the remaining ingredients.

3. Place the lid on, lock it and switch the pressure release valve to closed. Select WARM/CANCEL.

4. Select STEW (10mins). Once the timer gets to 0, the cooker will switch to Keep Warm automatically.

5. Switch the pressure release valve to open so as to release the steam. Once all steam is released, remove the lid.

Low Town Shrimp Boil

Servings: 6

Preparation time: 5 minutes

Cook time: 5 minutes

Ingredients

1/2 pound smoked sausage, cut into 1/2-inch slices

1 pound large fresh shrimp, in shells

1 can (14.5 ounces) chicken broth

1/3 cup white wine

1/4 teaspoon dried crushed red pepper

4 whole black peppercorns

1 bay leaf

5 to 6 whole new red potatoes

2 ears corn, cut into thirds

3/4 cup water

Directions

1. Place the inner pot in the Power Cooker. Add the wine, broth, corn, water, bay leaf, peppercorns, red potatoes and crushed red pepper in it

2. Cover and lock lid and turn the pressure release valve to closed. Select FISH/ VEG/ STEAM and select time button to 4 minutes. Once the timer gets to 0, the Power Cooker will switch to Keep Warm mode.

3. Switch the pressure release valve to open in order to release the steam. Remove the lid when the steam is fully released.

4. Stir in shrimp sausage. Cover cook for a minute.

Catfish In French Sauce

Serve over cooked rice. Have hot sauce available at the table for those who want it.

Servings: 4

Preparation time: minutes

Cook time: minutes

Ingredients

1½ pounds catfish fillets, rinse, pat dry & cut into bite-size pieces

2 teaspoons dried minced onion

1 14½-ounce can diced tomatoes

¼ teaspoon onion powder

¼ teaspoon garlic powder

1 teaspoon dried minced garlic

1 teaspoon hot paprika

1 medium green bell pepper, seeded & diced

¼ teaspoon dried tarragon

1 stalk celery, finely diced

Salt & freshly ground pepper, to taste

½ cup chili sauce

¼ teaspoon sugar

Directions

1. Add all the ingredients except fish to the Power Cooker and mix well. Stir the fillets gently into the tomato mixture.

2. Cover and lock lid and then switch the pressure release valve to closed. Press the button for the FISH/VEG mode and then adjust time to 5 Minutes. Once the timer gets to 0, the cooker will switch to Keep Warm mode by itself.

3. Switch the pressure release valve to open in order to release the steam. Remove the lid when the steam is fully released.

4. Take out the lid. Stir gently and add salt and pepper if needed.

Supreme Crab

Servings: 2

Preparation time: 2minutes

Cook time: 2 minutes

Ingredients

4 lbs King Crab Legs, broken in half at the joints

1/4 cup melted butter

3 lemon wedges

1 cup water

Directions

1. Add the broken crab legs and water to the inner pot of the Power Cooker.

2. Secure lid and switch the pressure release valve to closed. Select FISH/VEG/STEAM.

3. Once the timer gets to 0, the cooker will switch to KEEP WARM automatically. Switch the pressure release valve to open. Wait for the steam to release completely and then remove the lid.

4. Enjoy with melted butter and lemon wedges.

Lobster Delight

Servings: 2

Preparation time: minutes

Cook time: minutes

Ingredients

5 lobsters (1-lb total)

1/2 cup white wine

1/4 cup melted butter

1 cup water

Directions

1. Place the inner pot in the Power Cooker. Add to it, water, lobsters and wine.

2. Cover and lock lid on the Power Cooker, switch the pressure release valve to closed.

3. Select FISH/VEG and time button to 4 Minutes.

4. Once the timer gets to 0, the cooker will switch to KEEP WARM automatically. Switch the pressure release valve to open. Wait for the steam to release completely and then remove the lid.

5. Take out lobsters and enjoy dipped with melted butter.

Calamari In Tomato Stew

The dried herbs may be omitted if you have basil and fresh parsley. Simply stir 1 tablespoon of each of them into the calamari after quick-releasing the pressure.

Servings: 4

Preparation time: 10 minutes

Cook time: 15 minutes

Ingredients

2½ pounds calamari

2 tablespoons olive oil

1 small stalk celery, finely diced

1 small white onion, peeled & diced

1 small carrot, peeled& grated

3 cloves garlic, peeled& minced

1 28-ounce can diced tomatoes

1 teaspoon dried parsley

1 teaspoon dried basil

Salt & freshly ground black pepper, to taste

½ cup white wine

1/3 cup water

Directions

1. In your Power Cooker, sauté celery and carrots in oil for 2 minutes.

2. Stir in the onions; sauté again for 3 minutes. Stir in the garlic and then sauté it 30 seconds.

3. Clean, wash the calamari and pat dry. Add to the pot, together with the remaining ingredients.

4. Cover the Power Cooker, lock the lid then turn the pressure release valve to closed. Next, press the WARM/CANCEL button then choose SOUP/STEW (10mins).

5. When the time is up, the Power Cooker will switch to KEEP WARM automatically. Turn the pressure release valve to open.

6. Wait until the steam is released completely before opening the cover. Serve!

Creamy Crab

With the pressure cooker's moist environment, the flavors meld without drying the crabmeat out. Serve this tasty sauce over egg noodles, cooked rice, or toast together with a large tossed salad.

Servings: 4

Preparation time: 5 minutes

Cook time: 5 minutes

Ingredients

1 pound uncooked lump crabmeat

½ cup heavy cream

4 tablespoons butter

¼ cup chicken broth

½ stalk celery, finely diced

Salt& freshly ground black pepper, to taste

1 small red onion, peeled & finely diced

Directions

1. Place the inner pot in the Power Cooker. Melt the butter and then add the celery. Press STEAM to soften the celery and then add the onion; stirring and sautéing for 2-3 minutes.

2. Add the crabmeat and broth; stir.

3. Close lid and lock it. Switch the pressure release valve to closed. Select WARM/CANCEL. Select FISH/VEG/STEAM.

4. Once the cooker automatically switches to KEEP WARM, turn the pressure release valve to open to fully release steam. Remove the lid.

5. Stir in the cream carefully. Add salt and pepper as needed.

Quick 'n' Easy Paella

Servings: 6

Preparation time: 10 minutes

Cook time: 15 minutes

Ingredients

2 tablespoons olive oil

1 onion, chopped

2 cloves garlic, minced

1/2 cup clam juice

1 pound chicken breast tenders

1/2 cup chopped red pepper

1/2 cup chopped green pepper

1/2 cup of chopped tomatoes

1 (5 ounce) package of yellow rice

1/2 teaspoon oregano leaves, dried

1/4 teaspoon pepper

3/4 cup chicken of broth

1/2 pound deveined shrimp, fresh shelled

1/2 cup frozen peas

Directions

1. Pour the olive oil into the inner pot of the Power cooker and then heat.

2. Add garlic, chicken and onion. Press CHICKEN/MEAT to sauté for 3 to 5 minutes.

3. Add red pepper, green pepper, yellow rice, oregano, tomatoes, chicken broth, clam juice and pepper.

4. Close lid and lock it. Switch the pressure release valve to closed. Select WARM/CANCEL. Select RICE/RISOTTO (6mins).

3. Once the cooker automatically switches to KEEP WARM, turn the pressure release valve to open to fully release steam. Remove the lid.

4. Stir in peas and shrimp. Cover pot again. Lock lid. Select WARM/CANCEL. Press FISH/VEG (2mins). Once the cooker automatically switches to KEEP WARM, turn the pressure release valve to open to fully release steam. Remove the lid.

5. Serve and enjoy!

Fish Steaks With Olive Sauce And Tomato

Servings: 2

Preparation time: 5minutes

Cook time: 10 minutes

Ingredients

2 firm fish steaks, cut 1-inch thick

2/3 cup sliced mushrooms

2 tablespoons olive oil

2 cloves garlic, minced

1/2 cup chopped onion

4 Roma tomatoes, chopped

2 tablespoons capers, drained

1/4 cup chopped, pitted kalamata olives

2 tablespoons minced fresh parsley

1/8 teaspoon dried crushed red pepper

1/4 teaspoon salt

1/4 cup white wine

Directions

1. Insert the inner pot in the Power Cooker. Pour olive oil in it. Set it to FISH/VEG/STEAM and let the oil heat. Add garlic and onion and sauté for 2 to 3 minutes.

2. Add remaining ingredients, except fish and then stir.

3. Cover and lock the Power Cooker, and then switch the pressure release valve to closed. Set to WARM/CANCEL button. Choose FISH/VEG/STEAM and adjust time to 5 minutes.

4. Once the time is up, turn the pressure release valve to open. Wait until the steam is totally released before opening the cover.

5. Place fish in sauce and then spoon some sauce up over fish. Place lid on cooker. Press CANCEL. Set it to FISH/VEG/STEAM for 5 minutes.

SOUP MAIN DISHES

Beef Stock

Make a good beef stock in 1 hour. Freeze or refrigerate it or have it readily available for a real quick soup or sauce base.

Servings: 6 cups

Preparation time: 10 minutes

Cook time: 60 minutes

Ingredients

1 tablespoon olive oil

2 lb shanks, cubed 1 inch

1 lb beef bones

8 cups water

1 medium onion, chopped coarsely

1 large carrot, scraped & chopped coarsely

1 bay leaf

1/4 teaspoon ground black pepper or 6 peppercorns

1 celery stalk, coarsely chopped

1/2 teaspoon thyme

2 sprigs parsley

Salt to taste

Directions:

1. Place the inner pot into the Power Cooker and add oil. Press the CHICKEN/MEAT button. Once hot, add the beef and the bones and cook until browned. Remove and place on platter, draining off any excess fat.

2. Add the remaining ingredients. Cover and lock the Power Cooker, and then switch the pressure release valve to closed. Press the button for the WARM/CANCEL setting. Select SOUP/STEW and select time button to 60 minutes.

3. Once the timer gets to 0, the cooker will switch to Keep Warm automatically. Switch the pressure release valve to open so as to release the steam. Once all steam is released, remove the lid.

4. Line a strainer with damp paper towels or damp cheesecloth. Pour contents from the inner pot through it. Press with a wooden spoon to extract as much liquid as possible.

5. Let it cool then chill overnight. Remove any congealed fat that has accumulated on the surface.

Chicken Stock

An all natural and flavourful stock that is ready in just 30 minutes. Serve it simply as a broth or enjoy with noodles or rice, carrots, and celery. You can also use it in several recipes that call for stock or even broth.

Servings: 6 cups

Preparation time: 10 minutes

Cook time: 30 minutes

Ingredients

2 lb chicken parts

1 medium onion, peeled & halved

1 large carrot, scraped & cut in pieces

1 celery stalk, cut in pieces

2 sprigs parsley

1/4 teaspoon ground black pepper or 6 peppercorns

1 teaspoon thyme

2 bay leaves

Salt to taste

6 cups water

Directions:

1. Add all the ingredients in the inner pot of the Power cooker. Lock the lid in place and switch the pressure release valve to closed.

2. Select SOUP/ STEW and select time to 30 minutes. Once the timer gets to 0, the cooker will switch to Keep Warm automatically. Switch the pressure release valve to open so as to release the steam. Once all steam is released, remove the lid.

3. Line a strainer with damp paper towels or damp cheesecloth. Pour contents from the inner pot through it. Press with a wooden spoon to extract as much liquid as possible.

4. Let it cool then chill overnight. Remove any congealed fat that has accumulated on the surface.

Fish Stock

Use as base for fish soups or for sauces that go with fish dishes. When you prepare fish or shellfish, reserve the bones, shells and scraps. You could also buy very low-priced mild flavored whole fish from the fish market such as whiting; but remove the gills.

Servings: 6 cups

Preparation time: 10 minutes

Cook time: 25 minutes

Ingredients

2 lb fish and shellfish meat, bones, heads & shells

1 celery stalk, cut into pieces

1 carrot, scraped & cut in pieces

1 bay leaf

1 teaspoon thyme

4 peppercorns

2 sprigs parsley

1 onion, peeled &sliced

6 cups water

Salt to taste

Directions:

1. Add all the ingredients in the inner pot of the Power cooker. Lock the lid in place and switch the pressure release valve to closed.

2. Select RICE/RISOTTO and press the select button to 25mins. Once the timer gets to 0, the cooker will switch to Keep Warm automatically. Switch the pressure release valve to open so as to release the steam. Once all steam is released, remove the lid.

3. Let it cool then chill overnight or freeze until ready to use.

Vegetable Stock

There can use any type of vegetable for vegetable stock. Cook in your Power Cooker for a quick great stock.

Servings: 6 cups

Preparation time: 10 minutes

Cook time: 10 minutes

Ingredients

8 cups water

8 cups vegetables of choice, washed & roughly chopped

2 medium onions, peeled & quartered

1 to 2 garlic cloves, chopped

3 carrots, cut into chunks

1 to 2 parsnips, cut into chunks

4 celery ribs, cut into chunks

2 bay leaves

2 sprigs fresh thyme or oregano or 1/2 teaspoon dried

3 to 4 sprigs parsley

Salt, to taste

Directions:

1. Place water in the Power Cooker. Press CHICKEN/MEAT and bring to boil. Add all the ingredients, except salt.

2. Cover and lock the Power Cooker, and then switch the pressure release valve to closed. Press the button for the WARM/CANCEL setting. Select SOUP/STEW (10mins).

3. Once the timer gets to 0, the cooker will switch to Keep Warm automatically. Switch the pressure release valve to open so as to release the steam. Once all steam is released, remove the lid.

4. Let stock cool for a while and then strain well with a strainer to strainer to extract all of the liquid

5. Cool and chill for up to 3 days. Alternatively, freeze for up to 3 months.

Winter Spicy Veggie Soup

This dish is a treat, especially during the winter season. Don't you just love its spiciness?

Servings: 2-3

Preparation time: 15 minutes

Cook time: 40 minutes

Ingredients

1 cup celery, chopped

1 medium onion, chopped

1/2 cup carrots, chopped

1 fresh jalapeno (3inch long), chopped, with membrane &seeds removed

2 tbsp olive oil

1/2 tsp cumin seed

1 tsp coriander seeds

3 big russet potatoes, cubed, with peels on

2 ½ -3 quarts low sodium chicken broth

2 tablespoon chicken broth

4 cups water

1 tsp. ground cumin

1/4 tsp ground turmeric

2 tablespoon pickled jalapenos, chopped

Chopped cilantro to taste

Directions

1. Insert the inner pot in the Power Cooker and add oil. Press CHICKEN/MEAT and when it heats up, add cumin seeds and coriander seeds then heat until the coriander seeds pop.

2. Add the chopped carrots, celery, jalapeno and onion. Sauté about 5 minutes until onions are translucent.

3. Add the turmeric, pickled jalapenos and cumin. Add the potatoes and chicken broth.

4. Place the lid on, lock it and switch the pressure release valve to closed. Afterwards, press the button for the WARM/CANCEL setting. Press SOUP/STEW and the select button to 30 minutes.

5. Once the program ends, the cooker will switch to Keep Warm by itself. Turn the pressure release valve to open. Wait until the steam is released completely before opening the cover.

6. Add the chopped cilantro just before serving. Serve with good bread.

Portuguese Kale Soup

Collard greens can be used instead of kale, but this will change the flavor a bit.

Servings: 6

Preparation time: 1 hour: 15 minutes

Cook time: 20 minutes

Ingredients

2 15-ounce cans cannellini beans, rinsed & drained

4 cups chicken broth

4 large potatoes, peeled &diced

1 pound kale

1 tablespoon extra virgin olive oil

½ pound linguica or kielbasa, sliced

1 large yellow onion, peeled & thinly sliced

Salt and freshly ground black pepper, to taste

Directions

1. Trim the ribs from the kale and slice thinly into strips. Pour cold water into a bowl and soak the kale inside it for 1 hour then drain well.

2. Insert the inner pot in the Power Cooker. Add the oil, kielbasa or linguica and onions to it and stir well. Press the SOUP/ STEW/ button and cook until the onions are soft.

3. Add the drained kale, potatoes, broth, chicken and beans. Place the lid on, lock it and switch the pressure release valve to closed. Afterwards, press the button for the WARM/CANCEL setting.

4. Select SOUP/ STEW. Once the timer gets to 0, the cooker will switch to Keep Warm automatically.

5. Switch the pressure release valve to open so as to release the steam. Once all steam is released, remove the lid. Add salt and pepper to taste.

Chicken With Rice Soup

Servings: 6

Preparation time: 5minutes

Cook time: 6minutes

Ingredients

1/3 cup uncooked, long-grain rice

1-112 cups diced, cooked chicken

5 cups chicken stock

1/4 cup diced carrot

1/4 cup diced onion

1/4 cup diced celery

1 teaspoon salt

1/4 teaspoon pepper

Directions:

1. Place the inner pot into the Power Cooker and add the ingredients.

2. Cover and lock lid and then switch the pressure release valve to closed. Press the button for the RICE/RISOTTO (6mins). Once the timer gets to 0, the cooker will switch to Keep Warm mode by itself.

3. Switch the pressure release valve to open in order to release the steam. Remove the lid when the steam is fully released.

Fresh Vine-Ripened Tomato Soup

Enjoy the summery taste of fresh vine-ripened tomatoes celebrated in this soup. Herbs and sautéed onion or shallots may be added. Consider your dietary needs when choosing the dairy product you want added to the soup. Also consider how rich you like your soup!

Servings: 4

Preparation time: 10 minutes

Cook time: 10 minutes

Ingredients

½ teaspoon baking soda

8 medium fresh tomatoes

2 cups milk, heavy cream or half-and-half

1 cup water

Freshly ground black pepper, to taste

¼ teaspoon sea salt

Directions

1. Wash the tomatoes then peel, seed, and dice them. Add them along with the tomato juice to the inner pot of the pressure cooker. Add water and salt.

2. Cover and lock lid and then switch the pressure release valve to closed. Press the button for the FISH/VEG./STEAM (2 mins.) Once the timer gets to 0, the cooker will switch to Keep Warm mode by itself

3. Switch the pressure release valve to open in order to release the steam. Remove the lid when the steam is fully released.

4. Add the baking soda to the tomato mixture, stirring as you do. Once it's stopped foaming and bubbling, stir in the milk, heavy cream or half-and-half.

5. Cook until the soup is hot and thickened.

Summer Yogurt & Barley Soup

For a refreshing meal, this mint scented soup is best enjoyed well chilled on a hot summer day.

Servings: 6

Preparation time: 10 minutes

Cook time: 20 minutes

Ingredients

2 tablespoons butter

5 cups chicken stock

1/2 cup onion, finely chopped

3 cups plain yogurt, lightly beaten

4 tablespoons pearl barley, rinsed

3 tablespoons chopped fresh mint or 2 tbsp dried mint with1 tbsp minced fresh parsley

Salt &freshly ground pepper, to taste

Directions:

1. Add the butter to the inner pot of the Power cooker. Press CHICKEN/MEAT and heat. Add onion and sauté until wilted. Add barley and the chicken stock, stirring well.

2. Cover and lock, and then turn the pressure release valve to closed. Press the button for the WARM/CANCEL. Set it on CHICKEN/MEAT mode (15mins).

3. Once the timer gets to 0, the cooker will switch to KEEP WARM. Turn the pressure release valve to open. Remove lid once the steam is fully released.

4. Cool and remove to a container and chill. Stir in 2 tablespoons of the chopped mint and the yogurt. Add salt and pepper to taste, garnish with the rest of the mint. Serve and enjoy very cold.

Barley-Mushroom Soup

Enjoy this vegetarian soup. Substitute beef or chicken broth for the water if you want it to complement a meat entrée.

Servings: 6

Preparation time: 10 minutes

Cook time: 30 minutes

Ingredients

1 large carrot, peeled and diced

1 large sweet onion, peeled, halved, and sliced

2 tablespoons butter

½ cup pearl barley

2 stalks celery, diced

1 tablespoon olive or vegetable oil

2 cloves garlic, peeled and minced

8 ounces fresh mushrooms, cleaned and sliced

1 portobello mushroom cap, diced

1 bay leaf

6 cups water

2 tablespoons brandy or vermouth, optional

Salt & freshly ground black pepper, to taste

Directions

1. Insert the inner pot in the Power Cooker. Press SOUP/STEW and then melt butter. Add the carrot and the celery; and cook. Add the onion and sauté until it is soft and transparent.

2. Next, stir in the mushrooms and garlic; sauté for 5 minutes. Once the onion begins to turn golden and the mushrooms release their moisture, stir in the barley, bay leaf water, and vermouth or brandy if using.

3. Lock the lid into place; and then turn the pressure release valve to closed. Press the button for the WARM/CANCEL. Select SOUP/STEW then the button for Time until it reaches 20 minutes.

4. Once the timer gets to 0, the cooker will switch to KEEP WARM. Turn the pressure release valve to open. Remove lid once the steam is fully released.

5. Take out the bay leaf and discard. Add salt and pepper to taste. Serve.

Dry Split Pea Soup

Servings: 6

Preparation time: 15 minutes

Cook time: 15 minutes

Ingredients

1 onion, chopped

2 cups dry split peas

3 stalks celery, diced

1 Rapunzel vegetable bouillon cube, herbs included

1 teaspoon extra virgin olive oil

1/2 teaspoon granulated garlic

1/4 teaspoon black pepper

1 bay leaf

2 carrots, peeled& shredded coarsely

8 cups hot water

1 or 2 tablespoons of fresh lemon juice (optional)

Salt to taste

Directions

1. Remove dirt or small rocks from the split peas, place them in a strainer and then rinse well.

2. Place the split peas in the inner pot of the Power Cooker and add all the ingredients except the carrots. Stir to let the bouillon cube mix well with the hot water.

3. Secure lid and then switch the pressure release valve to closed. Press SOUP/ STEW on the button.

4. Once the program ends, the cooker will switch to Keep Warm by itself. Turn the pressure release valve to open. Wait until the steam is released completely before opening the cover.

5. Taste for seasonings; add salt and black pepper if necessary. Also, if needed, add 1-2 tablespoon freshly squeezed lemon juice to the soup to brighten the taste. Soup will thicken as it cools.

Caribbean Black Bean Soup

Like almost any bean dish, diced celery and carrot slices may be added to this soup once the onion is added.

Servings: 8

Preparation time: 20 minutes

Cook time: 55 minutes

Ingredients

8 ounces smoked sausage

3 cloves garlic, peeled & minced

½ pound bacon, chopped

1 large yellow onion, peeled & diced

1 green bell pepper, seeded & diced

2 teaspoons paprika

½ teaspoon ground cumin

1 tablespoon red wine vinegar

½ teaspoon chili powder

¼ teaspoon coriander

1 bay leaf

6 cups chicken broth or water

1 smoked turkey wing or smoked ham hock

1 pound dried black beans, soaked overnight, rinsed &drained

1/8 teaspoon dried red pepper flakes or cayenne pepper

½ cup dry sherry

115

Salt and freshly ground black pepper, to taste

Directions:

1. Place bacon in the inner pot of the Power Cooker. Select CHICKEN/MEAT and fry. Once the bacon starts to render its fat, add the green pepper, sautéing for 3 minutes.

2. Add the onion and stir. Dice or slice the smoked sausage and stir into the onion, sautéing until the onion is tender.

3. Add the garlic, stir and add the cumin, coriander, bay leaf, paprika, chili powder, water or broth, beans and turkey wing or ham hock.

4. Cover and lock, and then turn the pressure release valve to closed. Press the button for the WARM/CANCEL. Press the button for the SOUP/STEW and time selection button to 30 minutes.

5. Once the program ends, the cooker will switch to Keep Warm by itself. Turn the pressure release valve to open. Wait until the steam is released completely before opening the cover

6. Remove the turkey wing or ham hock and take the meat off of the bones; bring back meat to the Power Cooker. Remove bay leaf and discard.

7. Partially puree with a potato masher or immersion blender. Stir in the dried red pepper flakes or cayenne pepper, vinegar and sherry. Press SOUP/STEW and adjust time to 20 minutes.

8. Taste for seasoning; add salt and pepper as needed. If desired, adjust the chili powder, herbs and red pepper flakes or cayenne pepper.

Tasty Chowder With Potato& Bacon

This tasty Potato Bacon Chowder is so simple and remarkably fast. Just 5 minutes of actual cooking time!

Servings: 8

Preparation time: 15minutes

Cook time: 5 minutes

Ingredients

1 large onion, small diced

5 lbs. russet potatoes, peeled & cubed

1 lb. bacon, crisply fried & chopped rough

3 stalks celery, thinly sliced

4 cups chicken stock

1 clove garlic, minced

1 teaspoon ground black pepper

1 tablespoon seasoning salt

1 cup heavy cream

½ cup whole milk

¼ cup of butter

Sour cream, diced green onion and shredded cheddar cheese (for garnish)

Directions

1. Place the potato chunks in the inner pot of the Power Cooker. Add onion, celery, garlic, butter, salt and pepper, stirring to combine.

2. Add chicken stock and bacon to pot and stir. Secure lid and then turn the pressure release valve to closed. Press button to "Beans/ lentil" (5mins).

3. When the program is done, release the pressure by turning the pressure release valve to open then remove the lid.

4. Crush vegetables with a potato masher until it is a thick semi-smooth mash.

4. Add whole milk and cream, stir well. Serve topped with sour cream, sliced green onion and shredded cheddar.

Tofu &Winter Melon Soup
Servings: 6

Preparation time: 10 minutes

Cook time: 45 minutes

Stand Time: 24 hours

Ingredients

1 lb Pork bones

5 cups water

1 package tofu (700g)

1¾ lb. Winter melon

1 tablespoon olive oil

1 tablespoon green onion, chopped

2-3 slices of fresh ginger

2 cilantro rinsed & chopped

1/4 teaspoon ground black pepper

2 teaspoon salt

Directions

1. Place tofu in freezer overnight. Soak the pork bones with boiling water for 3-4 minutes, drain, wash and rinse pork bones with cold water.

2. Insert the inner pot in the Power Cooker. Place the pork bones inside and add 5 cups of cold water. Cover and lock, and then switch the pressure release valve to closed. Select SOUP/STEW and adjust cooking time 35 minutes.

3. Once the timer gets to 0, the cooker will switch to Keep Warm by itself. Switch the pressure release valve to open in order to release the steam. Remove the lid when the steam is fully released. Once cooled, refrigerate the pork stock

4. Defrost frozen tofu the next day. Peel off winter melon skin, rinse and slice. Cut defrost tofu into small pieces.

6. Press CHICKEN/MEAT button and heat olive oil in the Power Cooker, sauté ginger and chopped green onion for a minute, add the sliced winter melon and tofu, stir and cook 3-4 minutes.

7. Skim fat off of pork and then pour stock into the winter melon and tofu, bring to boil. Lower heat; add salt and black pepper and simmer until winter melon softens, that will be about15 minutes.

8. Divide soup into 6 bowls, scatter chopped cilantro over them and serve.

Sizzling Sour Soup

Servings: 4-6

Preparation time: minutes

Cook time: minutes

Ingredients

1 can (10-1/2 ounces) chicken broth

2 cans (10-1/2 ounces each) beef broth

1 tablespoon sesame oil

1 package (8 ounces) sliced mushrooms

1 pound pork cutlets, cut into 1/4 x 2-inch slices

8 green onions, sliced

1 can (8 ounces) bamboo shoots, drained

1/4 to 1/2 teaspoon dried crushed red pepper

1/4 cup cornstarch

1/4 cup soy sauce

2 tablespoons cider vinegar

Directions

1. Place the inner pot into the Power Cooker and add oil. Press the CHICKEN/MEAT button. Allow oil to heat and then add pork and brown on all sides. Add mushrooms and green onions and sauté for 3- 5 minutes.

2. Add beef broth, dried crushed pepper, bamboo shoots, and chicken broth.

3. Cover and lock lid and then switch the pressure release valve to closed. Press the WARM/CANCEL button. Select FISH/VEG/STEAM button

and time selector button to 4 Minutes. Once the timer gets to 0, the cooker will switch to Keep Warm mode by itself.

4. In a bowl, combine cornstarch and soy sauce and blend thoroughly. Stir the cornstarch mixture into the soup. Press STEAM; cook, uncovered and stir frequently until thickened. Add the vinegar and stir.

Tortilla Soup

Servings: 8-10

Preparation time: 10 minutes

Cook time: 10 minutes

Ingredients

1/3 cup vegetable oil

4 cloves garlic, peeled

2 onions, diced

1 can (15 oz) tomatoes, drained

3 quarts chicken broth

Tortilla chips

1 lb cheese, grated

Cilantro, chopped

Lime wedges (optional)

Directions:

1. Insert the inner pot in the Power Cooker. Sauté the onions and garlic in the oil until golden brown. Remove from cooker.

2. Add to a food processor or blender, add the tomatoes as well and then puree until smooth. Return to pot and then add the broth; heat to boiling.

3. Place the lid on, lock it and switch the pressure release valve to closed. Afterwards, press the button for the WARM/CANCEL setting.

4. Select SOUP/STEW (10mins).Once the timer gets to 0, the cooker will switch to Keep Warm by itself. Switch the pressure release valve to open in order to release the steam. Remove the lid when the steam is fully released.

5. Add the cilantro and season with salt. Place cheese and tortilla chips in bowls and pour the hot soup on top. If desired, serve with lime wedges.

One Pot Beef Bone Broth

Servings: 6-8 cups

Preparation time: 5 minutes

Cook time: 2 hours

Ingredients

3 pounds beef soup bones (plus two knuckle bones)

6 cloves garlic, peeled

3 stalks celery, washed & cut in two

4 large carrots, washed & cut in two

1 medium onion, cut into quarters

1 tablespoon apple cider vinegar

1 tablespoon kosher salt

6-8 cups of filtered Water (do not exceed the Power cooker's fill line)

Directions

1. Place all the ingredients in the Power Cooker. Lock lid in place and switch the pressure release valve to closed.

2. Press the button for SLOW COOK and select for 2 hours.

3. Once the program ends, the cooker will switch to Keep Warm by itself. Turn the pressure release valve to open. Wait until the steam is released completely before opening the cover.

4. Remove vegetables and bones with a slotted spoon and pass broth through a strainer. Enjoy!

Scotchy Broth
More like a soup than a broth. Enjoy it!

Servings: 4

Preparation time: 10 minutes

Cook time: 10 minutes

Ingredients

4 lamb shoulder chops

2 leeks, white part only

2 medium potatoes, peeled & diced

1 large carrot, peeled and diced

1/3 cup pearl barley

1 stalk celery, thinly sliced

Fresh parsley, minced, optional

Salt &freshly ground black pepper, to taste

6 cups water

Directions:

1. Dice the leeks (white part only), rinse thoroughly and drain. Add the diced leeks to the Power cooker and then add the lamb chops, carrot, barley celery, potatoes, salt, pepper and water.

2. Seal the lid and switch the pressure release valve to closed. Press SOUP/STEW (10mins). Once the program ends, the cooker will switch to Keep Warm by itself. Turn the pressure release valve to open. Wait until the steam is released completely before opening the cover.

3. Taste and add extra salt and pepper if necessary.

4. Transfer 1 lamb chop to each of 4 bowls. Ladle the soup over the meat. If desired, garnish with parsley.

Beef-Veggie Soup

Make Beef-Veggie Soup a tomato-based hearty dish by substituting two 15-ounce cans diced tomatoes for the beef broth.

Servings: 8

Preparation time: 10 minutes

Cook time: 21 minutes

Ingredients

1 3-pound chuck roast

1 10-ounce package frozen whole kernel corn, thawed

4 cups beef broth

7 large carrots

1 large sweet onion, peeled and diced

2 stalks celery, finely diced

8 ounces fresh mushrooms, cleaned and sliced

1 teaspoon butter, melted

¼ teaspoon dried rosemary

1 tablespoon extra virgin olive oil

1 clove garlic, peeled and minced

1 tablespoon dried parsley

1 10-ounce package frozen baby peas, thawed

6 medium potatoes, peeled and diced

¼ teaspoon dried oregano

1 bay leaf

1 10-ounce package frozen green beans, thawed

Salt and freshly ground black pepper, to taste

Tasty Substitutions:

1. To add more flavor to this soup, substitute several strips of bite-size pieces of bacon for the oil. The bacon bits will be absorbed into the dish and offer extra crunch and zing.

2. Alternatively, use canned French onion soup instead of some of the beef broth.

Directions

1. Peel the carrots, dice 6 of it and grate 1. Add the grated carrot, onion, celery, mushrooms, butter and oil to the Power Cooker.

2. Coat the vegetables in the oil and butter by stirring. Press STEAM and cook for 1 minute.

3. Stir the garlic in. Add the diced carrots, broth, parsley, oregano, potatoes, bay leaf, rosemary, pepper and salt.

4. Trim the roast of fat and cut it into bite-size piece. Now add it to the Power Cooker and the vegetables as well, stir.

5. Close lid and then switch the pressure release valve to closed. Select WARM/CANCEL. Now select CHICKEN/MEAT (15 mins).

6. Once the program ends, the cooker will switch to Keep Warm by itself. Turn the pressure release valve to open. Wait until the steam is released completely before opening the cover

7. Remove the bay leaf and discard. Stir in the peas, green beans and corn; cook for 5 minutes. Taste for seasoning

Soothing Soup Potato

Servings: 8 cups

Preparation time:15 minutes

Cook time: 30 minutes

Ingredients

1/2 teaspoon olive oil

2 slices bacon

1 onion, diced

1 cup of low sodium chicken broth

1 teaspoon minced garlic

2 1/2 lbs potatoes, peeled & chopped into 1- inch cubes

2 carrots, diced

1 tablespoon dried parsley

12 ounce can of evaporated milk

1 celery stalk, diced

2 cups of low sodium chicken broth

1 teaspoon dried Italian Seasoning

1 ½ teaspoons salt, to taste

Black pepper to taste

Dash of dried red pepper flakes

Directions

1. Place the inner pot into the Power Cooker and add oil. Press the CHICKEN/MEAT button and then add onion, garlic and bacon. Stir and sauté for 3-4 minutes.

2. Add 1 cup chicken broth, carrots, potatoes, red pepper flakes, celery, parsley and Italian seasoning. Stir. Secure lid, and switch the pressure release valve to closed. Afterwards, press the button for the WARM/CANCEL setting.

3. Press the SOUP/STEW button (10mins). Once the timer gets to 0, the cooker will switch to Keep Warm automatically. Switch the pressure release valve to open so as to release the steam. Once all steam is released, remove the lid.

4. Remove the bacon and discard. Now add 2 cups of chicken broth and evaporated milk. Puree with an emersion blender until desired creamy consistency is attained but leave chunks of potatoes.

5. Season with salt and pepper and stir to incorporate.

STEWS

Old South Chicken Stew

The sugar in this meal offset the tomatoes' acidity. With the aroma of the bacon fat, you will be transported back to a time when Southern cooks kept a bacon drippings container at the ready.

Servings: 8

Preparation time: 20 minutes

Cook time: 1 hour

Ingredients

1 10-ounce package frozen whole kernel corn, thawed

8 chicken thighs

3 tablespoons bacon fat

1 10-ounce package frozen okra, thawed & sliced

1 28-ounce can diced tomatoes

2 large yellow onions, peeled and sliced

1/4 teaspoon sugar

1 10-ounce package frozen lima beans, thawed

1/2 cup dry white wine or chicken broth

1 cup bread crumbs, toasted

Salt and freshly ground black pepper, to taste

3 tablespoons Worcestershire sauce

Hot sauce, to taste, optional

2 cups water

Directions

1. Insert the inner pot in the Power Cooker. Add the bacon fat. Press CHICKEN/MEAT and bring to temperature. Add 4 chicken thighs with the skin side down and fry until lightly browned.

2. Remove the fried chicken thighs and fry the remaining thighs. Bring back the first 4 fried chicken thighs to the pot and then add the tomatoes, water, wine or chicken broth, onions and sugar.

3. Cover and lock lid and then switch the pressure release valve to closed. Press CANCEL. Select SOUP/STEW. Once the timer gets to 0, the cooker will switch to KEEP WARM. Turn the pressure release valve to open. Remove lid once the steam is fully released.

4. Remove the chicken and remove the meat from the bones once it is cool enough to handle and discard the skin and bones. Shred meat and set aside.

5. Add the okra, corn and lima beans to the pot. Press CHICKEN/MEAT and adjust time to 40minutes, cook and simmer for 30 minutes. Stir in the bread crumbs, Worcestershire sauce and shredded chicken.

6. Simmer for 10 minutes, stirring infrequently to bring the chicken to temperature and to thicken the stew. Add hot sauce if desired and salt and pepper if needed.

Chicken, Lentil & Bacon Stew

Flavored –packed stews with French lentils, tender chicken legs, pancetta, onions, chicken stock, bay leaves and carrots for your evening delight.

Servings: 4

Preparation time: 20 minutes

Cook time: 10 minutes

Ingredients

2 1/2 pounds bone-in, skin-on chicken pieces

8 oz slab bacon or pancetta, cut into 1/2-inch

2 tablespoons extra-virgin olive oil,

2 medium carrots, peeled & chopped

1 medium onion, diced (about 1 cup)

2 bay leaves

2 teaspoons sherry vinegar

8 oz dried French lentils

12 sprigs parsley, leaves chopped roughly, stems tied together with kitchen twine

1 quart low-sodium chicken stock

Kosher salt

Freshly ground black pepper

Directions

1. Heat oil in the Power Cooker, using the CHICKEN/MEAT setting, until shimmering. Add bacon and cook until crisp around edges.

2. Now add the onions and cook, stirring, about 2 minutes, until softened but not browned. Add chicken stock, lentils, carrots, stems, bay leaves, parsley and chicken legs. Add salt and pepper and stir well to blend.

3. Cover and lock lid and then switch the pressure release valve to closed. Press WARM/CANCEL. Select SOUP/ STEW and then the button to adjust time until it reaches 20 minutes.

4. Once the program ends, the cooker will switch to Keep Warm. Turn the pressure release valve to open. Open the cover when all steam is released.

5. Use tongs to transfer chicken pieces to a bowl. Throw away the parsley stems. Press the Beans / Lentils setting and continue to cook and stir the lentils until thickened.

6. Meanwhile, shred chicken, discard bones and skin.

7. Now add chicken and vinegar into the beans, stirring well. Season with salt and pepper; add half of the chopped parsley stir well and then serve, topped with olive oil, parsley and sherry vinegar at the table.

Lamb Stew Africana

Cinnamon simmering in orange juice generates an appetizing aroma that fills the kitchen. Your family will love you more for this dish. Serve with couscous.

Servings: 6

Preparation time: 15 minutes

Cook time: 35 minutes

Ingredients

2 pounds boneless lamb shoulder

1 tablespoon olive or vegetable oil

1 cup dried apricots, quartered

2 cloves garlic, peeled and minced

1 large onion, peeled and diced

1/3 cup raisins

1 tablespoon fresh ginger, minced

1/3 cup blanched whole almonds

½ teaspoon ground cinnamon

¾ cup red wine

1/3 cup fresh mint leaves, packed

¼ cup fresh orange juice

Fresh mint leaves for garnish, optional

Salt and freshly ground pepper, to taste

Directions

1. In the pressure cooker, bring the oil to temperature. Trim lamb of fat and cut the meat into bite-size pieces.

2. Press CHICKEN/MEAT and then brown the lamb for 5 minutes each in batches. Set aside the browned lambs and keep warm.

3. Add the onion and sauté for 3 minutes. Add the garlic; sauté for 30 seconds. Stir in the browned lamb. Add raisins, apricots, ginger, almonds, wine, cinnamon, mint leaves and orange juice.

4. Cover and lock lid and then switch the pressure release valve to closed. Select CANCEL.

5. Press the button for the SOUP/STEW Stew mode and then adjust time to 20 Minutes. Once the timer gets to 0, the cooker will switch to Keep Warm mode by itself.

6. Switch the pressure release valve to open in order to release the steam. Remove the lid when the steam is fully released. If desired, garnish with fresh mint.

Herbed Chicken Stew With Dumplings

To stretch this meal to 6 or 8 main dish servings, serve over mashed potatoes.

Servings: 4

Preparation time: 25 minutes

Cook time: 35 minutes

Ingredients

¼ cup unbleached all-purpose flour

2½ cups chicken broth

8 bone-in chicken thighs, skin removed

2 tablespoons unsalted butter

2 stalks celery, finely diced

2 teaspoons dried parsley

½ cup dry white wine or water

1 large onion, peeled and diced

1 teaspoon dried thyme

12 ounces baby carrots, cut in half

1 bay leaf

1 recipe dumplings

½ teaspoon salt

¼ teaspoon freshly ground black pepper

Directions

1. Put the flour, salt and pepper in a large zip-closure plastic bag and shake to mix. Remove fat from chicken and add to the bag, seal and shake well to coat the chicken in the seasoned flour.

2. In the Power Cooker, press CHICKEN/MEAT and melt the butter. Add chicken thighs once the butter starts to bubble and brown on each side for 3 minutes. Transfer chicken to a plate

3. Add the celery and sauté for 2 minutes. Add the thyme and onion; sauté until the onion is softened. Stir in the parsley, carrots, broth, water or wine and bay leaf. Bring the browned chicken thighs (along with their juices) back to the pot.

4. Place the lid on, lock it and switch the pressure release valve to closed. Press CANCEL. Press SOUP/STEW (10mins).

5. Once the program ends, the cooker will switch to Keep Warm by itself. Turn the pressure release valve to open. Wait until the steam is released completely before opening the cover. Remove the bay leaf and discard.

6. Press CHICKEN/MEAT, Drop full teaspoons of the dumpling batter into the simmering stew. Cover and cook for about 15 minutes.

<u>Dumpling Batter</u>

1. In a mixing bowl, add 2 cups of unbleached all-purpose flour, 1 tablespoon of baking powder, and ½ teaspoon of salt. Stir well.

2. With two forks or a pastry blender, cut in 5 tablespoons of unsalted butter. Add 1 large beaten egg and ¾ cup buttermilk, stirring until the mixture comes together.

Tex-Mex South-Western Stew

A blend of the southwestern flavors of Texas and Mexico, this hearty Tex-Mex Stew is best served over rice together with an avocado salad and baked corn chips or cornbread.

Servings: 8

Preparation time: 10 minutes

Cook time: 50 minutes

Ingredients

1 7-ounce can green chilies

1 3½-pound English or chuck roast

2 14½-ounce cans diced tomatoes

2 tablespoons olive or vegetable oil

1 8-ounce can tomato sauce

1 green bell pepper, seeded and diced

1 large sweet onion, peeled and diced

6 cloves garlic, peeled and minced

1 teaspoon freshly ground black pepper

1 bunch fresh cilantro, chopped

1 tablespoon ground cumin

Cayenne pepper, to taste

2 tablespoons lime juice

2 jalapeño peppers, seeded & diced

Beef broth or water, optional

Directions

1. Trim fat from roast and cut meat into 1 inch cubes. Press CHICKEN/MEAT. Add the vegetable or olive oil to the Power Cooker. Add the beef and stir-fry until well browned.

2. Next, Stir in the tomatoes, chilies, onion, tomato sauce, garlic, bell pepper, black pepper, lime juice, cumin, jalapeño peppers and cayenne.

3. Add enough water or beef broth if needed, to cover the ingredients in the cooker.

4. Place the lid on, lock it and switch the pressure release valve to closed. Afterwards, press the button for the WARM/CANCEL setting. Press SOUP/STEW and adjust time to 40 minutes.

5. Once the program ends, the cooker will switch to Keep Warm by itself. Turn the pressure release valve to open. Wait until the steam is released completely before opening the cover.

6. Add the cilantro and serve immediately.

Clam Chowder Manhattan

The clams and the clams liquid will be salty, so it's best to wait until the chowder is cooked before adding any salt. Serve with dinner rolls, oyster crackers, or toasted garlic bread.

Servings: 6

Preparation time: 10 minutes

Cook time: 15 minutes

Ingredients

4 slices bacon

4 6½-ounce cans minced clams

4 large carrots, peeled and finely diced

2 stalks celery, finely diced

1 large sweet onion, peeled and diced

1 28-ounce can diced tomatoes

1 pound red potatoes, peeled and diced

2 cups tomato or V-8 juice

1/8 teaspoon dried oregano

½teaspoon freshly ground black pepper

1 teaspoon dried parsley

¼ teaspoon dried thyme

Sea salt, to taste

Directions

1. Drain the clams and set aside, reserving the liquid to add together with the other liquid.

2. Fry the bacon in the inner pot of the Power Cooker, using the CHICKEN/MEAT mode and crumble.

3. Next, add the carrots and celery; sauté 3 minutes. Add onion; sauté 3 minutes. Stir in the potatoes, stir-frying to coat the potatoes in the fat. Stir in undrained tomatoes, clam liquid, juice, thyme, parsley, pepper and oregano.

4. Cover and lock, and then turn the pressure release valve to closed. Press the button for the WARM/CANCEL. Select "Beans/Lentils".

5. Once the timer gets to 0, the cooker will switch to Keep Warm automatically. Switch the pressure release valve to open so as to release the steam. Once all steam is released, remove the lid.

6. Stir in the reserved clams. Press any cook button and bring to a simmer. Season to taste.

Rich Oxtails Stew

Servings: 4-6

Preparation time: 10 minutes

Cook time: 15 minutes

Ingredients

5 lbs oxtails

2 cups red wine

1 large onion, peeled & chopped

3 stalks celery, chopped

3 carrots, chopped

1 cup chopped tomatoes

1 small bunch parsley, chopped

1 clove garlic, peeled and chopped

1 cup water

Sugar to taste

Salt and pepper

Directions

1. Season the oxtails with salt and pepper.

2. Insert the inner pot in the Power Cooker and add in the oxtails.

3. Place the remaining ingredients, except the wine and water on top of the oxtails. Now pour the wine and water over all items.

4. Secure lid, and then switch the pressure release valve to closed. Select CHICKEN/ MEAT and then the button to select time until it reaches 40 minutes.

5. Let warm in the pot for 10minutes before opening the lid.

6. Season with salt, pepper, serve and enjoy.

Spanish Style Paella

Servings: 4

Preparation time: 20 minutes

Cook time: 30 minutes

Ingredients

2 cups rice, short or long grain

8 small-sized mussels or clams

2 tablespoons olive oil

1/2 lb halibut or monkfish cut in 1"pieces

1/2 lb shrimp, shelled

3 garlic cloves, minced

1 medium onion, chopped

1 tablespoon parsley, minced

1 pimiento, chopped

1/4 teaspoon paprika

1 small tomato, skinned, seeded& chopped

4 cups, clam juice, fish stock or chicken broth

1/4 teaspoon saffron

1/2 cup peas

Directions:

1. Insert the inner pot in the Power Cooker. Press CHICKEN/MEAT.
Pour 1 cup water and bring to a boil. Add the mussels and cook until open.
Dispose off half of the shell and transfer the mussels to a platter.

2. Dry the inner pot. Add oil and heat, and then sauté the fish and the shrimp until just cooked. Add to the platter and cover with foil tightly.

3. To the Power Cooker, add the onion and garlic and sauté the onion until the onion is wilted. Add the pimiento, paprika, parsley and the tomato, stirring and cooing 3 minutes.

4. Add the rice and stir to coat thoroughly. Pour in the stock, add the peas and then the saffron, and bring to a boil.

5. Finally, cover and lock lid and then switch the pressure release valve to closed. Press the button for the WARM/CANCEL setting.

6. Select RICE/RISOTTO and adjust time to 8 minutes. Once the timer gets to 0, the cooker will switch to Keep Warm automatically.

7. Let sit, for another 4 minutes with lid closed. Switch the pressure release valve to open so as to release the steam. Once all steam is released, remove the lid.

8. Add the reserved mussels, fish and the shrimp, stirring well.

Wild Mushroom Risotto

Servings: 4-6

Preparation time: 5 minutes

Cook time: 15 minutes

Ingredients

8 oz fresh mushrooms, coarsely chopped

2 cups Arborio rice

4 cups chicken or vegetable stock

1/4 cup dry vermouth or cooking wine

2 tablespoons shallots, coarsely chopped

1/4 cup Parmesan cheese, grated

3 tablespoons olive oil

Salt and pepper to taste

Directions:

1. Insert the inner pot in the Power Cooker. Press CHICKEN/MEAT. Add shallots to hot olive oil and simmer 3 minutes, stirring often but do not let brown.

2. Add the mushrooms and rice, and stirring constantly 1 minute. Stir in cooking wine and stock. Cover and lock the Power Cooker, and then switch the pressure release valve to closed. Press CANCEL.

3. Select RICE/RISOTTO and adjust time to 9 minutes. Once the program ends, the cooker will switch to Keep Warm by itself. Turn the pressure release valve to open. Wait until the steam is released completely before opening the cover.

4. Stir well and then add the grated Parmesan cheese. If desired salt and pepper.

Pineapple & Cauliflower Mixed Rice

Every kid will love this pineapple and veggie mixed rice because of its pleasant aroma and delicious taste.

Servings: 6

Preparation time: 5 minutes

Cook time: 30 minutes

Ingredients

2 cups rice

1 cauliflower minced

1/2 pineapple or ½ can pineapple, minced

1 teaspoon salt

2 teaspoons oil

Directions

1. Add enough water to the inner pot of the Power Cover. Add all ingredients and then switch the pressure release valve to closed.

2. Select RICE/RISOTTO. Once the timer gets to 0, the cooker will switch to KEEP WARM. Turn the pressure release valve to open. Remove lid once the steam is fully released.

3. Once done, serve and enjoy.

Confetti Rice

Brown rice makes for a healthy, fiber-rich dish so use instead of white rice, if desired.

Servings: 6

Preparation time: 15 minutes

Cook time: 15 minutes

Ingredients

1 cup long-grain white rice, rinsed & drained

3 cups frozen mixed vegetables, thawed

1 small red onion, peeled& diced

2 cloves garlic, peeled & diced

3 tablespoons butter

¼ cup fresh lemon juice

1 tablespoon ground cumin or herb blend

1 14-ounce can chicken broth

½ teaspoon black pepper, freshly ground

½ teaspoon salt

Directions

1. In the Power Cooker, melt the butter, set to medium heat. Add the onion and sauté until soft. Add the garlic and then sauté it for 30 seconds.

2. Add the rice, stirring to coat in the butter; sauté until the rice becomes translucent. Add all other ingredients. Stir well.

3. Secure the lid into place; switch the pressure release valve to closed. Press CANCEL. Select RICE/RISOTTO and adjust time to 9minutes.

4. Once the program ends, the cooker will switch to Keep Warm by itself. Turn the pressure release valve to open. Wait until the steam is released completely before opening the cover.

5. Fluff rice with a fork. Taste and add seasoning if necessary.

Bow Tie Pasta In The Pressure Cooker
Enjoy this quick, easy and tasty meal – it's just perfect for a weeknight meal!

Servings: 4

Preparation time: 5 minutes

Cook time: 20 minutes

Ingredients

16 oz. Bow-Tie Pasta

1 pound lean ground sausage (or chicken sausage)

1 tablespoon of olive oil

1 onion, finely chopped

28 oz. can crushed tomatoes in puree

2 cloves garlic, crushed

1 teaspoon of dried basil

1/4 teaspoon of salt

1/8 teaspoon of red pepper flakes

3 ½ cups of water

Directions

1. Add olive oil to inner pot of Power Cooker. Press CHICKEN/MEAT and sauté garlic, onion and sausage until onion is tender and meat loses its pinkness.

2. Add the rest of the ingredients and stir. Secure the lid into place; switch the pressure release valve to closed. Press CANCEL. Select RICE/RISOTTO (6mins).

3. Once the timer gets to 0, the cooker will switch to Keep Warm automatically. Let sit, for another 4 minutes with lid closed. Switch the pressure release valve to open so as to release the steam. Once all steam is released, remove the lid.

4. Stir mixture. Select STEAM, stirring constantly, until the pasta is tender. Season with salt and pepper.

Succulent Coconut Rice

Enjoy this succulent rice dish. It is really good served with a curry entrée.

Servings: 4

Preparation time: 5 minutes

Cook time: 10 minutes

Ingredients

1 cup extra long-grain white rice, rinsed &drained

2 tablespoons butter or vegetable oil

½ cup unsweetened coconut, flaked or grated

¼ cup currants

2¼ cups water

1/8 teaspoon ground cloves

½ teaspoon ground cinnamon

1 teaspoon anise seeds

½ teaspoon salt

Directions

1. Place the inner pot into the Power Cooker and add oil. In the pressure cooker, bring the oil or butter to temperature over medium heat. Add the rice, stirring to coat it in the fat.

2. Add the water, coconut, cinnamon, currants, anise seeds, cloves and salt.

3. Cover and lock lid and then switch the pressure release valve to closed. Press the button for WARM/CANCEL. Select RICE/RISOTTO (6mins).

4. Once the program ends, the cooker will switch to Keep Warm by itself. Turn the pressure release valve to open. Wait until the steam is released completely before opening the cover.

5. Fluff rice with a fork. Drain off excess moisture. Add seasoning as needed. Serve!

Rice With Sausage And Potato

Fast, easy and convenient; this one-pot dish is for everyone.

Servings: 8

Preparation time: 15 minutes

Cook time: 20 minutes

Ingredients

2 cups of long grain rice

2 lean Chinese sausages, cut thinly into slices

1½ tbsp olive oil

5 small yellow potatoes (400g), peeled & cut into small pieces

1½ tablespoon green onion, finely chopped

3-4 slices of fresh ginger

1¼ tsp salt

3 cups water

¼ tsp chicken broth mix

1/6 teaspoon ground black pepper

1 tbsp green onion, finely chopped

Directions

1. Rinse sausages and potatoes under cold water; drain. Add olive oil to Inner pot of the Power Cooker. Press CHICKEN/MEAT. Sauté green onion and ginger for 2-4 minutes. Add sausages and cook 1-2 minutes. Add potatoes and cook 1-2 more minutes.

2. Add rice and combine thoroughly. Add lsalt, ground black pepper, water and chicken broth mix.

3. Place the lid on, lock it and switch the pressure release valve to closed. Afterwards, press the button for the WARM/CANCEL setting. Select RICE/RISOTTO (6 mins).Once the timer gets to 0, the cooker will switch to Keep Warm automatically.

4. Switch the pressure release valve to open so as to release the steam. Once all steam is released, remove the lid.

5. Add a tablespoon of chopped green onion, mix thoroughly and then serve.

Lime Rice With Chipotle's Cilantro

Servings: 4

Preparation time: 5 minutes

Cook time: 6 minutes

Ingredients

1 cup long grain rice

1 tablespoon fresh lime juice

2 tablespoons vegetable oil

3 tablespoon fresh chopped cilantro

1 teaspoon salt

1 1/4 cups water

Directions

1. Insert the inner pot in the Power Cooker. Add the rice, 1 tablespoon oil, salt and water to the pressure cooker. Stir.

2. Cover and lock lid and then switch the pressure release valve to closed. Select RICE/RISOTTO (6mins). Once the program ends, the cooker will switch to Keep Warm by itself. Turn the pressure release valve to open. Wait until the steam is released completely before opening the cover.

3. Combine lime juice, chopped cilantro and1 tablespoon oil in a medium bowl. Add rice and toss until well mixed.

Pasta With Tuna & Capers (Pasta Al Tonno)
Servings: 4

Preparation time: 2 minutes

Cook time: 10 minutes

Ingredients

16 oz fusilli pasta, uncooked

2 5.5oz cans tuna, packed in olive oil

1 tablespoon olive oil

3 anchovies

1 garlic clove

2 cups tomato puree

1½ teaspoons salt

2 tablespoons capers

Water

Directions

1. Add oil, anchovies and garlic to the inner pot of the Power Cooker. Press RICE/RISOTTO until the garlic cloves are just about to turn golden and the anchovies begin to break up.

2. Add the tomato puree and salt; stir well. Add the pasta, and then empty in one tuna can (5 oz) stirring to coat the dry pasta. Level out the pasta evenly and add water to cover.

3. Press the SOUP/STEW. Once the program ends, the cooker will switch to Keep Warm by itself. Turn the pressure release valve to open. Wait until the steam is released completely before opening the cover.

4. Add in the last 5oz can of tuna, mix and sprinkle with capers. Serve!

Rice Pilaf

Enjoy a distinctive Middle Eastern flavored meal enhanced by the pine nuts and raisins in this recipe.

Servings: 4

Preparation time: 5 minutes

Cook time: 10 minutes

Ingredients

1 cup rice

2 tablespoons canola oil or butter

2 tablespoons onion, minced

2 tablespoons pine nuts

2 cups chicken or vegetable stock

2 tablespoons golden raisins

1 tablespoon minced parsley or 1 teaspoon dried

1 teaspoon thyme

Salt and ground pepper to taste

Directions:

1. Insert the inner pot in the Power Cooker. Heat oil or melt butter and sauté onion until softened. Add the rice and coat well with the butter. Add the rest of the ingredients and bring to a boil.

2. Cover and lock lid and then switch the pressure release valve to closed. Press the button for WARM/CANCEL. Select RICE/RISOTTO (6mins)

3. Once the timer gets to 0, the cooker will switch to Keep Warm by itself. Switch the pressure release valve to open in order to release the steam. Remove the lid when the steam is fully released.

4. Dry in oven before serving.

One Pot Basmati Rice
Servings: 4

Preparation time: minutes

Cook time: minutes

Ingredients

2 cups of Basmati Rice

3 cups of Water

Directions

1. Rinse the rice in a strainer, cover and soak in fresh water for 15 minutes.

2. Strain rice; add to the inner pot of the Power Cooker and add water. Secure lid and switch the pressure release valve to closed. Select RICE/RISOTTO.

3. When the program is done, release the pressure by turning the pressure release valve to open; open the lid.

Sweet Brown Rice Risotto

The white grape juice concentrate makes the rice real sweet. If you' want to keep it absolutely savory, do away with the white grape juice concentrate and use ¼ cup of white wine and 2½ cups of water instead.

Servings: 8

Preparation time: 15 minutes

Cook time: 30 minutes

Ingredients

2 cups short-grain brown rice, rinsed& drained

2 medium leeks

3 tablespoons butter

1 small fennel bulb

½ teaspoon salt

1½ teaspoons freshly ground or cracked black pepper

2¾ cups water

¾ cup Fontina cheese, grated

1 tablespoon frozen white grape juice concentrate

Directions:

1. Cut the leeks lengthwise into quarters, and then slice into ½-inch slices; wash well, drain, and dry.

2. Clean, trim the fronds from the fennel and chop. Dice the bulb.

3. In the Power Cooker, Press CHICKEN/MEAT and melt the butter over medium heat. Add the fennel and leeks; sauté for 1minute.

4. Add the rice, stir-fry into the almost wilted leeks until the rice starts to turn golden brown. Add the water, white grape juice concentrate and salt.

5. Cover and lock the Power Cooker, and then switch the pressure release valve to closed. Select WARM/ CANCEL and then Select SOUP/ STEW and then the button for Time Adjustment button until it reaches 20 minutes.

6. Switch the pressure release valve to open in order to release the steam. Remove the lid when the steam is fully released.

7. Fluff rice with fork. Stir in the fennel fronds, cheese, and pepper. Taste and add more salt if necessary. Serve!

Risotto With Peas
An easy and fast wonderful Mediterranean dish to savor.

Servings: 4

Preparation time: 5 minutes

Cook time: 15 minutes

Ingredients

2 tablespoons canola oil

1 small onion, finely chopped

1 cup short-grain rice

2 1/4 cups chicken or vegetable stock

1 cup frozen peas

1/3 cup Parmesan cheese

1/8 teaspoon pepper

Directions:

1. Insert the inner pot in the Power Cooker. Press the button for CHICKEN/MEAT. Heat 2 tablespoons of oil and sauté and stir onion until soft. Add rice and sauté until light brown. Add the stock and peas, stirring well.

2. Cover and lock lid and then switch the pressure release valve to closed. Press the WARM/ CANCEL button. Press RICE/RISOTTO and adjust time to 9 minutes.

3. Once the timer gets to 0, the cooker will switch to Keep Warm mode by itself. Switch the pressure release valve to open in order to release the steam. Remove the lid when the steam is fully released.

4. Let sit until cheese melts. Stir thoroughly and serve. (Alternatively, cook the veggies separately and mix them into the risotto at the end).

Mediterranean Tuna Noodle Delight

Servings: 4

Preparation time: 10 minutes

Cook time: 15 minutes

Ingredients

8 oz dry wide egg noodles

1 can tuna fish in water, drained

1 tablespoon of oil

1 can (14 oz) diced tomatoes with garlic, basil, and oregano (un-drained)

½ cup of chopped red onion

¼ teaspoon of salt

1 jar (7.5 oz.) marinated artichoke hearts, drained with liquid saved, then chopped up.

1-1/4 cups of water

Crumpled feta cheese

Fresh or dried parsley, chopped

1/8 teaspoon pepper

Directions:

1. Place the inner pot into the Power Cooker and sauté red onion using the CHICKEN/MEAT setting.

2. Add the tomatoes, dry noodles, salt, pepper and water to pot. Place the lid on, lock it and switch the pressure release valve to closed. Afterwards, press the button for the WARM/CANCEL setting. Press SOUP/STEW (10mins).

3. Once the timer gets to 0, the cooker will switch to Keep Warm by itself. Switch the pressure release valve to open in order to release the steam. Remove the lid when the steam is fully released.

4. Add artichokes, tuna, and the reserved artichokes liquid, sauté and stir continuously until hot.

3. Enjoy topped with feta cheese and parsley.

VEGETABLE MAIN DISHES

Pressure-Steamed Artichokes

Servings: 2-4 as an appetizer

Preparation time: 5 minutes

Cook time: 30 minutes

Ingredients

2 medium-sized whole artichokes (about 5 ½ ounces each)

1 cup water

1 lemon wedge

Directions

1. Rinse the artichokes and remove any outer leaves that are damaged. Trim off the stem and the top of the artichokes carefully. Rub the cut top with lemon to prevent browning.

2. Next, Set a steamer tray into the Power Cooker, place the artichokes on top, and add water. Lock lid into place, and then turn the pressure release valve to closed. Select SOUP/STEW and adjust time to 20 minutes.

3. Release the pressure by turning the pressure release valve to open then open the lid. Remove the artichokes and serve warm with your preferred dipping sauce.

Easy Creamy Mashed Cauliflower

Creamy mashed cauliflower is easy to make and taste great.

Servings: 2

Preparation time: 5 minutes

Cook time: 10 minutes

Ingredients

Medium head of cauliflower, cut into smaller pieces, leaves and stem removed and the rest cut into sections of florets

2 cloves garlic

1/2 cup unsweetened almond milk

3tablespoons of nutritional yeast

1/2 teaspoon of freshly ground black pepper

1/2 teaspoon salt

1 cup water

Directions

1. Put the steamer tray in the Power Cooker and pour the water in. Add the cauliflower.

2. Secure lid, turn the pressure release valve to closed and then press the STEAM button (2 mins).

3. When program is completed, release the pressure and open the lid.

4. Remove the cauliflower and blend in the blender. Add the remaining ingredients and blend till the cauliflower is homogenized, soft and pliable.

Purple Yam Barley Porridge

Purple yam is loaded with anti-oxidants and high in fiber. Its purplish color makes exceptional exotic porridge.

Servings: 12

Preparation time: 10 minutes

Cook time: 45 minutes

Ingredients:

1 purple yam (about 300g)

3 tablespoons pearl barley

3 tablespoons pot barley

3 tablespoons buckwheat

3 tablespoons glutinous rice

3 tablespoons black glutinous rice

3 tablespoons black eye beans

3 tablespoons red beans

3 tablespoons Romano beans

3 tablespoons brown rice

1/6 tsp baking soda (optional)

Directions:

1. Clean yam, remove skin and cut into cubes. Wash the rice, beans and barley.

2. Insert the inner pot in the Power Cooker. Add the washed rice, beans and barley. Place the yam cubes and the baking soda in it and fill water to the maximum limit.

3. Place the lid on, lock it and switch the pressure release valve to closed. Set on SOUP/STEW mode and adjust cooking time to 50 minutes.

4. When the program is done, release the pressure and open the lid. Serve plain or with blue agave syrup, sugar or honey.

Barley Casserole

Servings: 4

Preparation time: 10 minutes

Cook time: 45 minutes

Ingredients:

1 cup pearl barley, uncooked

1 1/2 cups eight vegetable juice

1/8 teaspoon pepper

1 large carrot, chopped

1 bell pepper, green or red & chopped

1 onion, chopped

1 green or red bell pepper, chopped

2 garlic cloves, minced

1 cup mushrooms, chopped

1 - 1 1/2 cups stock, chicken or vegetable

1/4 cup toasted pine nuts or chopped walnuts

Directions:

1. Add all ingredients to the inner pot of the Power Cooker. Do not add the nuts.

2. Lock the lid in place and switch the pressure release valve to closed. Set on Beans / Lentils mode and select cooking time to 30 minutes.

3. When the program is done, release the pressure completely by turning the pressure release valve to open and then open the lid.

4. Serve, sprinkled with nuts.

Curry & Chickpea stuffed Acorn Squash
Servings: 2

Preparation time: 25 minutes

Cook time: 30 minutes

Ingredients

¼ cup of brown rice, (washed and soaked for 30 minutes)

¾ cup dry chickpeas

1 teaspoon oil

½ teaspoon of cumin seeds

½ cup red onion, chopped

4 garlic cloves, finely chopped

1 green chili, minced

½ inch ginger, minced

¼ teaspoon turmeric

½ teaspoon garam masala

½ teaspoon dry mango powder (amchur) or ½ tsp extra lime juice

½ teaspoon lime juice

2 small tomatoes, chopped

1 cup chopped greens, loosely packed (rainbow chard or spinach)

¼ to ½ teaspoon cayenne

1 small acorn squash, halved & deseeded

½ teaspoon or more salt

2 cups water

Paprika, cilantro, and black pepper (for garnish)

Directions

1. Soak the chickpeas overnight but soak the brown rice for 30-40 minutes before preparation.

2. In a Power Cooker, add oil and heat using the CHICKEN/MEAT mode. Add cumin seeds and cook 1 minute until fragrant and change color.

3. Add onions, ginger, chili, garlic and a pinch of salt. Cook until translucent, about 5 minutes. Add spices, mix well and then add tomato, greens and lime juice, cook 4 to 5 minutes or until the tomatoes are saucy.

4. Add water to deglaze if needed. Add salt, chickpeas, cayenne, rice and 2 cups of water, mixing thoroughly.

5. Add one half or both halves of the squash, placing squash in a steamer tray over the chickpea mixture. Secure lid. Switch the pressure release valve

to open. Select WARM/ CANCEL and then select CHICKEN/MEAT (15mins). Let the pressure release and open the lid.

6. Remove the steamer plate. Taste chickpea rice stew for salt and spice and adjust where necessary. Fill squash with the chickpea rice mixture and then garnish it with black pepper and cilantro. *Serve!*

Green Beans & Bacon
Serving: 4-8

Preparation time: 10 minutes

Cook time: 15 minutes

Ingredients

8 cups fresh green beans

1/2 lb bacon, thickly sliced

1/8 cup sugar, more or less to taste

Salt and pepper, to taste

Directions

1. Chop and brown bacon in the inner pot of the Power Cooker, using the CHICKEN/MEAT mode, until crispy then set aside to a platter.

2. Wash beans and add water to just cover it.

3. Secure lid into place and then turn the pressure release valve to closed. Press CANCEL. Set cooking mode to Beans / Lentils (5mins).

4. When the program is done, release the pressure by turning the pressure release valve to open then open the lid

5. Add the bacon including the grease and the sugar. Stir, close lid and set cooking mode to Beans / Lentils again.

6. Season with salt and pepper then serve.

Simple Pinto Beans

Servings: 4

Preparation time: 5 minutes

Cook time: 40 minutes

Ingredients

1 pound dry pinto beans

1 bunch cilantro stems, tied with butcher's twine

1 small onion, finely chopped

7 cups water

1 garlic clove, minced

1 1/2 teaspoons salt

1 teaspoon ground cumin

Directions

1. Add all the ingredients in the Power Cooker. Cover, lock lid and switch the pressure release valve to closed. Select CHICKEN/MEAT and press the select button to 40 minutes.

2. Once the program ends, the cooker will switch to Keep Warm by itself. Turn the pressure release valve to open. Wait until the steam is released completely before opening the cover.

Red Lentils With Sweet Potato

Servings: 2

Preparation time: 5 minutes

Cook time: 5 minutes

Ingredients:

1/2 cup red lentils, rinsed

1 sweet potato, peeled and chopped

1 small or medium onion, peeled & diced

1 tablespoon nutritional yeast flakes

1/2 tsp cinnamon

1/4 tsp garlic powder

1/4 tsp chipotle chili pepper powder

2 tablespoons of Sushi Rice Vinegar

1 1/2 cups water

Directions

1. Place all ingredients in the inner pot of the Power Cooker. Stir to combine.

2. Cover and lock lid and then switch the pressure release valve to closed. Press the button for BEANS / LENTILS (5mins).

3. When the program is done, release the pressure by turning the pressure release valve to open then open the lid.

4. Serve hot with over broccoli.

Black Eye Peas Delight
Simple and just perfect!

Servings: 4

Preparation time: 5 minutes

Cook time: 5 minutes

Ingredients

1/2 lb bag black eyed peas, dried

1 tablespoon olive oil

3 ½ cups broth or water

1 ½ cups diced frozen onion

1 tablespoon oregano

1 1/2 teaspoons salt

Directions:

1. Add all to your Power Cooker. Cover and lock the Power Cooker, and then switch the pressure release valve to closed.

2. Press the BEANS / LENTILS button. Once cook, turn the pressure release valve to open. Let steam release completely before opening.

3. Serve and enjoy!

Potatoes With Fresh Parsley

Servings: 4

Preparation time:10 minutes

Cook time: minutes

Ingredients

2 lbs potatoes, peeled &sliced

1 cup water or chicken stock

2 Tbsp fresh parsley, minced

4 Tbsp butter, cut into cubes

Salt& pepper to taste

Directions

1. Place potatoes and parsley into Power Cooker and stir. Season with salt and pepper. Add water or chicken broth and top with butter.

2. Lock lid securely and switch the pressure release valve to closed. Select BEANS /LENTILS (5mins).

3. Once the timer gets to 0, the cooker will switch to Keep Warm by itself. Switch the pressure release valve to open in order to release the steam.

4. Remove the lid when the steam is fully released. *Serve!*

Summer Boiled Peanut Salad

Servings: 4

Preparation time: 10 minutes

Cook time: 20 minutes

Ingredients

2 medium tomatoes, chopped

1 pound raw peanuts in shell, shelled

1/2 cup diced green pepper

1 bay leaf

2 tablespoons olive oil

1/2 cup sweet onion, diced

1/4 cup hot peppers, finely diced

1/4 cup celery, diced

2 tablespoons fresh lemon juice

3/4 teaspoon salt

1/4 teaspoon of freshly ground black pepper

2 cups water

Directions

1. Skin peanuts by blanching them in boiling salt water for a minute and then drain. Remove skins and discard.

2. Add peanuts to inner pot of Power Cooker; add the 2 cups of water and bay leaf. Place the lid on, lock it and switch the pressure release valve to closed.

3. Select SOUP/ STEW and adjust time to 20 minutes. Once the timer gets to 0, the cooker will switch to Keep Warm automatically.

4. Switch the pressure release valve to open so as to release the steam. Once all steam is released, remove the lid. Drain.

5. In a large bowl, add together peanuts and vegetables. Add the lemon juice, oil, salt and pepper, mixing well.

6. Pour over the salad mixture, tossing to combine.

White Beans The New Orleans Style
Servings: 8

Preparation time: 20 minutes

Cook time: 45 minutes

Ingredients

1 pound of dried great northern beans

1 small green pepper

4 minced cloves garlic

1 medium onion

2 ribs celery

1 tablespoon soy sauce (or gluten-free tamari)

1 teaspoon dried thyme

1/2 teaspoon white pepper

1 teaspoon dried oregano

1 teaspoon salt

Tabasco, to taste

Hickory smoked salt, to taste (optional)

2 bay leaves

Directions

1. Soak beans overnight or quick-soak by putting them into the Power Cooker with water to cover them by just three inches. Secure lid and cook for 1 minute.

2. Drain soaking liquid. Place the beans into the Power Cooker. Add 5 cups water to it and heat, uncovered.

3. Meanwhile, in a food processor or by hand, chop all vegetables fine, adding to the pressure cooker as you chop. Add other ingredients except Tabasco and the hickory smoked salt, if using.

4. Check the water level in the Power Cooker and add 1 more cup if there isn't enough water to cover all the ingredients by 1 inch.

5. Cover lid, and then switch the pressure release valve to closed. set on BEANS / LENTILS and then adjust time to 12 Minutes.

6. Once the timer gets to 0, the cooker will switch to Keep Warm mode by itself. Switch the pressure release valve to open in order to release the steam. Remove the lid when the steam is fully released.

7. Check beans for doneness. If beans are still tough, cover and cook press STEAM (2mins). If tender, add Tabasco and smoked salt and then sauté uncovered until the liquid reduces and the cooking water starts becoming more like a sauce.

8. Stir frequently so they don't burn. If the liquid still seems watery after about 20 minutes, remove bay leaf and blend part of the beans with an immersion blender. Add salt to taste. Serve over hot rice with hot sauce placed on the table.

Spinach& Lentil Night

Servings: 6

Preparation time: 10 minutes

Cook time: 20 minutes

Ingredients

2 tablespoon of olive or coconut oil

1 large red or yellow onion, chopped

1 teaspoon ground turmeric

1 teaspoon ground cumin

3 cloves garlic, minced

1 teaspoon ground coriander

1/4 teaspoon dried cayenne pepper

1.5 cups of red lentils and/ or yellow split peas

1/2 teaspoon salt

1 large tomato, cut into 6-8 wedges

Handfuls (about 4 cups) of spinach

1/4 cup fresh cilantro, chopped (optional)

2 tsp butter (optional)

3 cups water

Directions

1. Add the olive or coconut oil to the Power Cooker. Using the CHICKEN/MEAT mode, sauté onions until soften and translucent and

then add the garlic. Cook 1 minute until fragrant. Select WARM/CANCEL to turn off heat.

2. Add the coriander cumin, cayenne and turmeric, mixing well. Add the lentils, tomato wedges, water and salt and then add to the onion mixture, stirring well.

3. Place the lid on, lock it and switch the pressure release valve to closed. select   Press the button for the SOUP/STEW mode (10mins). Switch the pressure release valve to open in order to release the steam. Remove the lid when the steam is fully released.

4. Remove and throw away tomato skins; whisk lentils to emulsify and smash the tomato wedges against the side of the pot. Add the spinach, cilantro and butter if using, stirring to mix. The residual heat will quickly wilt the spinach.

5. Serve with naan, brown rice, topped with fresh cilantro and plain yogurt.

Mashed Potatoes With Green Onions

Servings: 4

Preparation time: 10 minutes

Cook time: 10 minutes

Ingredients

2 pounds Yukon gold or russet potatoes, peeled & cut into 1/2 inch thick slices

4 green onions, trimmed & thinly sliced

3/4 cup milk

4 tablespoons butter

2 teaspoons kosher salt

Directions

1. In the inner pot of the Power Cooker, melt butter over medium heat; sauté the green onions and potatoes. Sprinkle with the salt, toss to coat with the butter and pour the milk into the pot, stirring well.

2. Lock the lid and then turn the pressure release valve to closed. Select BEANS/LENTILS and adjust time to 7 minutes.

3 Once the timer gets to 0, the cooker will switch to KEEP WARM. Turn the pressure release valve to open. Remove lid once the steam is fully released.

4. Mash the potatoes. If too thick, add a little more milk. Add more salt if needed.

DESSERTS

Caribbean Rice Pudding

Arborio rice is combined with coconut milk and studded with pineapple pieces in this colorful rice pudding.

Servings: 8

Preparation time: 5 minutes

Cook time: 5 minutes

Ingredients:

1 tablespoon coconut oil

1 cup of Arborio rice

1 1/2 cups water

1/4 teaspoon salt

1/2 cup of sugar

1 (14-ounce) can coconut milk

2 eggs

1/2 teaspoon of vanilla extract

1/2 cup of milk

1 can pineapple tidbits, drained & halved

Directions:

1. Insert the inner pot in the Power Cooker. Add rice, coconut oil, water and salt to it.

2. Secure lid and then switch the pressure release valve to closed. Set on STEAM and then adjust time to 3 Minutes. Once the timer gets to 0, the cooker will switch to Keep Warm. Switch the pressure release valve to open. Remove the lid when the steam is fully released.

3. Add sugar and coconut milk then stir to combine.

4. In a small bowl, whisk together the eggs, 1/2 cup milk and the vanilla. Pour the mixture through a fine mesh strainer into the Power Cooker.

5. Press "*sauté or brown*" and cook with constant stirring, until the mixture is bubbly. Turn the Power Cooker off and add the pineapple tidbits, stirring well.

6. Pour into serving dishes and refrigerate to chill. The pudding will solidify as it cools.

7. Serve, topped with whipped cream and toasted coconut.

Tea Poached Pears

Servings: 4

Preparation time: 10minutes

Cook time: 10minutes

Ingredients:

2 slices lemon

3 Earl Grey tea bags tied together

4 firm pears, peeled not cored,

1/4 tsp vanilla essence

2 cups water

2 cinnamon sticks

1/2 cup sugar

Directions

1. In the Power Cooker, mix together water, lemon, sugar, tea bags, vanilla essence and cinnamon sticks and then simmer until the sugar dissolves.

2. Next, place the pears in the Power Cooker even if they don't stand upright. Cover lid; switch the pressure release valve to closed. Set on FISH/ VEG/ STEAM mode and press the select time button for 10 minutes.

3. Once cooked, switch the pressure release valve to open in order to release the steam. Remove the lid when the steam is fully released.

4. Use a skewer to check the level of the softness of the pears. If more cooking is needed, replace lid and then press STEAM to pressure cook for two more minutes.

4. Transfer the pears to a large bowl with a slotted spoon and discard the tea bags. Boil sauce to lessen until it is syrupy. Drizzle over the pears and serve with cream, custard or ice cream.

5. (To make in advance, cool the pears and place in a container. Pour the syrup over the pears and then seal container.

6. To serve, remove pears from container, heat in the microwave for 2 minutes on medium setting. Heat the syrup separately for 1 minute in the microwave).

Easy Fruit Jam

Servings: 4 cups

Preparation time: 5 minutes

Cook time: 20 minutes

Ingredients:

1 cup water

4 cups blackberries, raspberries, strawberries

3 teaspoons pectin

1 teaspoon lime or lemon juice

1 cup sugar

Directions:

1. Combine the fruit and water in the Power Cooker.

2. Secure lid and then switch the pressure release valve to closed. Set on SOUP/STEW (10mins). Once the timer gets to 0, the cooker will switch to Keep Warm. Switch the pressure release valve to open. Remove the lid when the steam is fully released.

3. Mash the fruit with a potato masher. Add the pectin, sugar and lemon juice or lime. Press "sauté" and let simmer8-10 minutes, while stirring occasionally, until the jam starts to stick to the spoon or simply press the 'soup/stew' button.

4. Spoon the jam into jars. Let it cool and then cover with airtight lid.

Chocolaty Rice Pudding
Servings: 6-8

Preparation time: 5minutes

Cook time: 8 minutes

Ingredients

1 1/2 cups Arborio rice

200g (7oz) dark chocolate, chopped

1/3 cup caster sugar

6 cups milk

1 tsp vanilla extract

2 oz butter

1/4 teaspoon ground chili, optional

Directions

1. Put the rice, butter, milk, sugar and vanilla, into the Power Cooker and stir.

2. Cover and lock, and then turn the pressure release valve to closed. Cook for 8 minutes using the RICE/RISOTTO button and adjusting accordingly.

3. Once the timer gets to 0, the cooker will switch to KEEP WARM. Turn the pressure release valve to open. Remove lid once the steam is fully released.

Cob Corn Plain

You'll love this dish if you're watching your calories! This tastes delicious without any salt or butter.

Servings: 4

Preparation time: 2 minutes

Cook time: 2 minutes

Ingredients

1 lime, quartered

4 ears fresh sweet corn, shucked

Freshly ground black pepper, to taste

½ cup water

Directions

1. Place the steamer tray in the Power Cooker and then place the corn on the tray. Pour the water in.

2. Lock the lid and then turn the pressure release valve to closed. Press the button for STEAM. When the program is done, release the pressure by turning the pressure release valve to open.

3. Transfer to 4 serving plates. Squeeze a wedge of lime juice over corn and season each ear of corn with grind black pepper.

The End

Made in the USA
Middletown, DE
02 January 2017